To Michelle, with love on your fifteenth birthday.

Mom & Dad

(Celebrated in Pinner, Middx., England.)

YESTERDAY'S
SUNSHINE

AYLESBURY ROAD CRICKET TEAM

BACK ROW Soapy Sudds, Giggy Jones, Udders Huxley, Monkey Mercer, Marrow Woodhams, Stinker Smellet, Hairy Carter.

FRONT ROW Sports Master, Pedler Reid, Patsy Morgan (me), Mousey Hewet, Spider Morrison, Tidler Thomset, Head Master.

YESTERDAY'S SUNSHINE

REMINISCENCES OF AN EDWARDIAN CHILDHOOD

Verne Morgan

BAILEY BROTHERS & SWINFEN LTD
FOLKESTONE

Published in Great Britain by
Bailey Brothers and Swinfen Ltd
1974

SBN 561 00240 1

Printed in Great Britain by
Kingprint Limited, Richmond, Surrey

To Rowley, Nellie and Fred.

The amusing characters and vagaries
of Edwardian life, as seen through
the eyes of a small boy.

Contents

1

Please may I leave the room

"You can't possibly remember that", my Mother kept saying, "You were little more than a baby".

But I did remember it. I could, in fact, recollect with perfect clarity visiting the baker's shop in Peckham Rye and choosing the cake for my second birthday. A bitterly cold December morning with icicles hanging everywhere.

"Better than those pea-souper fogs", Mother had said when we started off.

It was six days before Christmas, the shops were loaded and people milling everywhere. I watched wide-eyed. Life was very exhilarating. It was a world of horses and cobble stones. Postmen, with their funny hats, a peak at both ends, and huge sacks on their backs, delivering the Christmas mail. Occasionally a telegraph boy would hurry by on his red bicycle. Errand boys at a slower pace would whistle the latest music-hall tune as they trundled their ware to its destination.

I felt very small. It was a world of big feet and long flowing skirts that were lifted up from behind when ladies

1

crossed the road.

"Choose", I heard my Mother say. I turned and gazed at the colourful display in the baker's shop window. I pointed to one that took my fancy, but Mother said no, it was too dear. We went inside and settled for a much smaller one. It was exciting, but I was secretly disappointed. One month before, my brother, four years my senior, had also had a birthday cake. It had been made at home by Mother's own hands. A large cake covered in sugar icing, and six wax candles which he had to blow out. He'd also had a party in the evening and we'd all gone into the back garden to let off some fireworks, A lot of other boys had come and one girl who, like me, watched the fireworks from the safety of the scullery window.

But Mother said not to worry. I would have my birthday party at Christmas. And for the rest of my youthful days that was the annual procedure. It was the luckless mishap of being born so close to the festive season.

Despite that it was a memorable day. In the afternoon I was taken for a ride on top of a bus. I had been on a bus before but never on top. My legs were too short to negotiate the perilous winding stairway. But the bus conductor, on being told it was my birthday, said he'd got six kids of his own and gathered me up in a flying angel and whisked me up before Mother could say nay. The great thing in those days was to sit on the front seat next to the driver. One could imagine the reins in one's own hands and, if the driver liked the look of you, he might exchange a cheery word and might even let you hold the whip. The high spot of all was if the bus pulled into a coaching station and the two horses were exchanged for a different pair. You felt you travelled much faster after that.

Christmas came and went, and the next bit of excitement came when I was "breeched". Little boys in those days were dressed much the same as girls for the first couple of years. Then the transition from petticoats to trousers was the crowning event in a boy's life. I was taken into the sitting room and stood on the ottoman. There I was divested of my girlish attire and yanked into something more masculine. It was, in fact, a miniature sailor suit, with a round straw hat that had ribbon dangling down the back. My Father and Mother stood back, the better to view me, and they laughed and they laughed. My Father said I looked like a little monkey. I felt terrible. It was my first experience of hurt feelings and punctured pride. I loved monkeys, certainly. Didn't I give them my sweets when I passed them in the street sitting on top of their barrel organs? I thought monkeys delightful, but I didn't want to look like one. However, there I was, a fully fledged male member of adult society, ready and willing to take my place in the world.

The following Sunday I was packed off to Sunday School with my Brother. He was an old hand at the game, but to me it was a fascinating new world. I learnt to sing "Jesus wants me for a Sunbeam" in a high treble voice, and I learnt all about God. Very soon I acquired a fervour for religion. But I got things a little out of plumb. I thought God's name was Mister Hallerby. (Didn't we all chant it in the Lord's Prayer? —"Our Father, we chant in heaven, Hallerby thy name"). And I got some rather odd ideas about heaven. I imagined it to be like an enormous railway signal box, with hundreds and thousands of levers, and God dashing about tugging at them to make us do the things we do. If ever I did something I was later ashamed of, I put the blame firmly on God's shoulders. I had every intention of going straight up to him on the final day of judgement and saying, "I'm sorry Mister Hallerby, I know I've committed a lot of sins, but if you hadn't pulled the wrong levers I should never have done it".

My ardent faith in God and religion stayed with me until I was almost grown up. Then quite suddenly one day it took a shatter. I had always taken part in the annual school sports. I was a moderately fast runner, and regularly and without fail, I went down on my knees by the side of my bed on the eve of the races and asked God to help me to win one of them. I never got in the first three, in fact, I never even got in one of the finals. But, in my last year at school, when I was about thirteen, I completely forgot to pray. I don't know why, I

3

just forgot. And the next day I won, not only the hundred yards, but also the coveted two hundred and fifty. I knew then that henceforth I could trust no one.

On my third birthday, I set fire to the curtains. My parents, who were usually hard up, had pooled their resources and bought me a large wooden horse called a Dobbin. I took him to my heart immediately I saw him. He had a sad face. I lugged him about all day, wouldn't let him out of my sight. When evening fell I thought he might like to have a look at the bright lights outside. So I took him into the front bedroom. This room was lit by an open gas jet which operated on a swivel near the window. As I wriggled my way through the lace curtains, there was a curious noise like a "whoof". The next moment I was enveloped in flames. My Mother rushed in, ripped the curtains down and squeezed out the flames with her bare hands.

It was terrifying. Her poor hands were badly burned, she just stood there shaking and shaking them. Little bits of charred curtain floated about the room. She kept looking at me but she couldn't speak.

"It wasn't Dobbin's fault", I heard myself saying in a hoarse whisper. "I bent down to give him a bunk up so's he could look out der window, and den I turned round, and I taught to myself 'What der duce is dat?'" Then my Mother did a strange thing. She laughed. And I was forgiven.

Only the upper class and those who had got on a bit could afford to illuminate their rooms with the new electric light. We had incandescent in the sitting room and an oil lamp in the kitchen. Other than that candles were used with the one exception of the front bedroom with its dangerously open jet. So you can imagine the thrill when, one day, we were invited to tea in a place that boasted electric light in the drawing room.

My Father, like most men of that era, was politically minded. There were just the two parties, Liberals and Conservatives. Father was a radical. He even used to get up and make speeches at open-air meetings, much to Mother's discomfort. On account of these activities, he got friendly with a Mr. Rowlands who was organising a campaign for the once-a-week half-day closing of shops. Mrs. Rowlands wrote, "Come for a cup of tea, and see our new electric light".

So off we went.

We were shown into the drawing room (a new name to us this), and there it was! Hanging from a flex in the middle of the room. It was capped with a thing like a large saucer. On a wall close by was a large brass ball with crinkles, and in the centre of it was a tiny thing they called a switch. "Watch", said Mrs. Rowlands, and she walked over and gave the switch a flick. The bulb immediately lit up. "Isn't it wonderful?" smiled Mrs. Rowlands, "No matches, no lighted tapers, no smoke".

My Mother said it was magic and Father said he hoped it wouldn't throw the miners out of work. I was transfixed, and later allowed to switch it on and off, just to show how easy it was. A breathtaking experience, only superseded by the good quality of the Madeira cake.

It was a boys' world that I had come into. Boys were the thing. The birth of a baby girl was greeted with politeness but without enthusiasm. The eldest boy in particular was placed on a pedestal. My Brother was no exception to the rule. Not only my parents but all the relations (and there were a whole lot of them) idolised him from the day he was born. My Father doted on him. I felt a little bit inferior. I always knew Mother loved me, but Father, well I was a bit frightened of him. A strict disciplinarian, a firm believer of the spared rod spoiling the child.

So I greeted the future with mixed feelings when Mother said one night she was taking Brother Fred to have his first violin lesson, and that as they might be late home she had instructed Father to put me to bed. I was apprehensive, and I don't think Father was very pleased about it either. I'd never been alone with my Father before. He got me undressed and I hopped into bed. After that he seemed at a loss, so he made me a bowl of hot bread and milk. I sat up in bed drinking it and we sort of sized each other up. He seemed quite happy really. He strolled around the room humming and whistling to himself, occasionally studying me with his head on one side. I had a notion he was trying to come to a decision. Anyhow, he collected the empty bowl, kissed me goodnight, and crept quietly out of the room. Not half as bad as I'd expected. I snuggled down into the warm bedclothes.

I loved my Father, I reflected, nearly as much as I loved my Mother. Then, full of tranquility and warm bread and milk I dozed off to sleep.

The next morning Mother had me on the carpet. "After Father kissed you goodnight, did he leave the house?" she demanded. Mother was obviously in a temper. How to cement the new bond of friendship with my Father and yet be loyal to my Mother?

"Did he leave you alone in the house?" my Mother reiterated again and again. I did a quick think. A case for compromise, I decided.

"Well", I said at length, "I didn't actually hear him go out, but I did notice when he tucked me up he had an artful grin on his face".

My Father must have been a very restless man. He had a multiplicity of jobs and never stayed long at any of them. Consequently we were continously on the move. One of the few nice pieces of furniture we possessed was a solid oak wardrobe with a beautifully carved ornamental fresco. This had to be screwed on and it took a long time. Father got so fed up screwing it on and then unscrewing it again, he ultimately propped it up with a bit of wood and left it semi-suspended all ready for the next move. I think it was this constant change of surroundings that gave birth to my phenomenally long memory.

I was still but in my second year when I saw my first airborne balloon. Secretly I had always cherished a belief that if I jumped with sufficient confidence from a high building, I would be able to fly like a bird. I did, in fact, put this theory into practice some years later, on the beach from a high railing at the seaside, with disastrous results. However, there it was, up there with people in it. Two to be exact, and they peered over the side and waved to us. After that it became almost a common sight, but when I was six I saw my first airship. This was a thrill indeed. We were having sprats for tea. Mother used to get them from a dear old man who hawked them up the street on a home-made barrow (a wooden box on two wheels) and they were delicious. "Lots of flour and fry them lightly", she used to say. We took no notice of this strange noise at first. Then we heard someone outside shouting, "Look, it's an airship". We all piled out, and there it was! Right overhead, with its propeller in the front buzzing away like one o'clock. The gasbag was shaped something like a squat cigar, and it had a thing hanging from its middle that looked like a large laundry basket. Everybody was in the street and they stared at it spellbound. We watched it chug its way over the rooftops.

"What *will* they think of next?" Mother said, and the lady next door said she didn't know what the world was coming to. We then went indoors to finish our sprats.

Later that evening my Uncle Fred and Aunty Emily turned up. They had come to discuss the latest phenomena. My Father, who said he was in the know, assured us that in Germany they were turning these things out as fast as they could, and that if war should ever come between us they would fly over and drop bombs on us from above. My Mother said if that was the case we'd lose. My Father, a loyalist to the backbone, said the British Soldier was a match for anyone. He would shoot them down. My Mother demurred. She said she'd been told on very good authority the hardest thing for a soldier to do was to lie on his back and fire his rifle into the air.

We were all petrified! I had visions of German Soldiers with spiked helmets and waxed moustaches leering over the side of their airships and lighting the fuses of big round bombs so cunningly timed that they exploded as they hit the ground.

Father reassured us. He said the British Soldier was the finest in the world. A crack shot! "A target as large as an airship? He couldn't miss!"

"No", said Mother, "and he couldn't reach".

Father rose to his feet. You could almost hear Rule Britannia and Land of Hope and Glory exuding from his brain. He happened to know he said (and he lowered his voice in case of enemy agents) that the British Government were building aeroplanes as fast as they could go. If war came, said he, the British Soldier would be trained to go up and shoot these airships down from close range. My Mother said she had never heard anything so ridiculous.

"How could a man", she asked, "steer an aeroplane with one hand and fire a rifle with the other?"

My Father, who had just sat down, stood up again. He said it was a proved technological fact that an aeroplane could fly much higher than an airship, and the British Soldier would fly above the Germans and drop bombs on his gasbag from aloft.

But my Mother said, in a small voice, it was also a proved fact that if a man went up in the air over a mile his lungs would burst and he would die. To which my Aunt Emily added, "If man was meant to fly he would've been born with wings".

After that Father and Uncle Fred took themselves off for a drink and my Mother and Aunt Emily fell to discussing the latest style in hats as advertised at the Bon Marché.

But war didn't come, not on that occasion. King Edward went over himself in person (to use my Father's phrase) and averted the disaster. The picture papers next morning were full of photographs of the King sitting by the side of the Kaiser in an open carriage riding through the streets of Berlin in an endeavour to create goodwill between the two nations.

"What courage!" my Mother said. "He's more than a King, he's a man!"

Soon after that my Aunty Maud came to stay with us. She was my favourite aunt. Much like my Mother in looks and temperament. I had once spent a week's holiday at her lovely house in Brixton. Brixton in those days was a rather high class neighbourhood. She was only recently married to a Reg. Lewis, who was a close relation to a famous Solicitor of that time, and he had provided her with a charming home.

Stylishly modern, with armchairs covered in damask, anti-macassars as a protection against gentlemen who soaked their hair in Macassar Oil, wax flowers under a glass dome, and a hand-woven Japanese screen to keep out the draughts. In a corner was the latest innovation — a phonograph, with a handle that you wound up like a mechanical toy. I also vividly remember an enormous brass gaselier hanging from the ceiling. It was the last word in modernity, not lit by matches but by a small pilot flame known as a bypass.

I spent a week on my own in this paradise. Just me and Aunty Maud; my Uncle Reg was away travelling. He was a representative for Mazawatee Tea and had a good job. By the end of the week I had decided I liked my Aunty Maud better than anyone else in the world, with the exception of my Mother. She was a good cook too.

And now here she was, my favourite Aunt come to spend a whole long week with us. My Father at work, my Brother at school all day, just my Aunt, my Mother and me.

Then, quite unexpectedly, a sensational piece of news! King Edward was to pass by quite close to our road the very next day. My Aunty Maud, like my Mother, was touchingly devoted to the royal family, and King Edward in particular. It was very much a romantic attraction. At the mention of King Edward's name, they went all of a dither. I don't suppose either of them slept much that night; and the next morning, limp with suppressed excitement, they set about dressing themselves 'fit for a king'.

My Aunty Maud wore a dinky little hat with a bunch of geraniums at the side. Mother looked stunning in a dark blue velveteen frock, cut on the cross, which she had made herself. I was poshed up in my new knickerbocker suit with the enormous lace collar and a poe-hat to match. I hated myself in it, but Aunty Maud assured me I looked simply topping.

We set off in plenty of time and, as always at these royal occasions, we waited and waited. It seemed hours. Then all at once we heard in the distance the sound of ecstatic cheering.

"He's coming", shouted Mother.

"Long live the King", they all yelled.

"Hooray! Hooray!"

We all surged forward. The King's carriage passed so close to us we could have touched him. Mother craned her neck forward and smiled right bang into his face. He raised his hat and smiled back.

I suppose it was the spontaneous release of pent up emotion that did it. I felt a curious kind of explosion in my lower regions, and there was the sound of much wet splashing on the pavement. My Aunty Maud shifted uncomfortably, but Mother, still smiling at the King said, "Don't look down, he's left the room in his trousers".

2

Pongo and panto

In due course Father got a job with Lovibond's, delivering beer from a wagon drawn by two sturdy horses. His branch was situated in the Acton area, so we moved there. In point of fact, we were half way between Acton and Ealing, and we shared a house with a woman called Mrs. Harlow. She essayed the impression of having seen better days. Her voice was strident and her manner somewhat theatrical. She had the extraordinary gift of pitching her cadence in both a high key and a low key at the same time. Quite fascinating if you hand't too sensitive an ear. And she wasn't all that fussy about her aitches.

"Do you know, my dear", she addressed my Mother on our arrival, "that you have come to live in the healthiest part of all London?"

My Mother said she didn't know.

"Oh yes", she went on in her ear-piercing voice, "it's a well known fact. You see, Acton h'acts on the 'ealth, and Ealing 'eals you!"

My Mother didn't like her. Especially when she noticed

strange men roaming about the place late at night. She averred you couldn't trust people who 'put the pot on', and Father, a practical man if ever there was, arrived at the conclusion she was 'doing a bit on her own'.

We didn't stay very long with Mrs. Harlow (Father had a slightly different name for her), because as luck would have it, the premises over the Lovibond Off-Licence in Acton's main thoroughfare fell vacant. It was offered to my Father and we moved in. It was a large building and we had two rooms at the top which we couldn't furnish. One was fitted up as a playroom and the other just used for storage.

Mrs. Harlow's quip about the district being so healthy proved her wrong. We'd hardly been at the new place five minutes before I went down with scarlet fever. My Mother was determined I should not go to hospital. A bed was taken upstairs into the store room and Mother and I were isolated away up there on our own and didn't see anybody else for about six weeks.

She wore an enormous kind of nightgown which I presume was impregnated in some way, and a disinfectant sheet was hung outside between us and the staircase. My Father used to leave tasty bits of food and things on the landing, on the other side of the sheet, and my Mother would rescue them and bring them in for us to share.

It was a trying time, but in a sense I enjoyed it. I had got Mother to myself. She used to cut out little monkeys from orange peel and stick them round the oil lamp. 'Christmas decorations' she called them. For some reason these little monkeys she made held great sentiment for me. But I was terribly lonely. I supposed I missed my Brother. It was in one of these little fits of depression that my Mother hit on the idea of making me a doll. She made it out of an old wooden spoon. It was not a pretty doll, it wasn't meant to be. It was a 'boy's doll', with a funny face and it emanated a sense of humour. It was large as dolls go, for the spoon was a big one, and this acted as the backbone. It was padded with odd bits of material, shaped into human form, and Mother painted a face on it in ink. It was a remarkably creditable achievement.

It had an extraordinary fetching little mouth which looked for all the world as though it was saying, "Phew! what a pong". So he was christened 'Pongo' on the spot. It somehow took on a personality all its own and we boys contrived to invest it with a soul. This doll, in fact, played quite a major part throughout the whole of our childhood life. Pongo developed a unique and fascinating dialect. It was a particular style of speech which is difficult to describe on paper. It had a low whistling note down the nose for certain consonants and a laboured kind of drawl on the vowels. It spoke, of course, through us and one great advantage was that no one but us could do it. My Mother had a go on one or two occasions but failed dismally and as for Father, well he never knew what the hell it was all about. As time went on my Brother and I almost always addressed each other in the third person, through Pongo, using the Pongo voice. Even when we reached maturity this nonsense went on, right up to my Brother's final illness. And it was always a laugh. The most tragic moments of our lives were often allayed through Pongo's observations. When my Brother went, Pongo folded up too, for there was no one else to talk him. He grew up with us, literally, for each year Mother would "re-do" him. He had a complete covering sewn over the old one, so that year by year he got bigger and bigger. Eventually, the head and face had to be re-moulded too — a kind of face lift — because his body was getting out of proportion to the size of his head. But whatever his size, he was the same old Pongo, still passing the same sultry remarks. Sometimes, being downright vulgar. By the time I left school, he was about four feet high, and his last "re-do" of all left him sporting a pair of long trousers and my left-off jacket. I never knew quite what happened to his body. By that time there was a world war hotting up, and Mother never said, but, as I mentioned before, the voice lingered on. He was still with us in spirit tho' his wooden spoon was somewhere underground. (Or was it? With the shortage of things as the war progressed, it probably came back into service in some way or other).

Anyhow, back to Acton and the sick room. I spent my

fourth birthday and Christmas in bed. My Brother used to sit on the top stair and tell me about the world down below.

"We've got balloons and coloured paper things all strewn across the ceiling", he would say breathlessly. "Wish you could see them".

I tried to picture it in my mind. "Wish I could", I rejoined.

"And we've got a Christmas pudding with a sprig of holly on it, and Dad's going to soak it in brandy and set fire to it". I fancied Mother pricked her ears up at this.

"Sounds nice", was all I could say.

"It is. It's absolutely ripping! Wish you were here".

"Wish I was", I said again.

"Goodbye then".

"Goodbye. Come again tomorrow".

This became a daily routine; I would listen to the clock on the mantelpiece ticking away, waiting and hoping he wouldn't be long. Then his school holiday drew to an end and he came up the stairs less often. My Father, of course, made the upstair journey quite frequently, but he spoke mostly to my Mother about household affairs, finishing sometimes with a cheery little word for me and bidding me be a good boy and that it wouldn't be long now.

At last I reached the convalescent stage and was out of quarantine. Brother Fred was allowed to come up into the room and brought all his Christmas presents. A monkey-up-a-stick, a toy theatre, and a thing which you set light to and a great snake plopped out. Life once more became absorbing and when Father said he was taking us all to see a pantomime my excitement knew no bounds.

I had never been inside a theatre before, but my Brother had, and he told me exactly what to expect. I got a graphic description of the raised stage and the sunken orchestra pit in front with the band playing and the conductor waving his baton. He enacted the lady dancers and mimicked their mannerisms.

I saw it all.

I visualised the whole affair as taking place in the Miss

Tyler's drapery shop next door. The Misses Tyler who ran it were two elderly spinsters. They wore black and smelt faintly of moth balls. They were very charming and used to fuss over me quite a bit. I liked them but they were homogeneously fuddy-duddy. Their shop was quite the largest place I had ever been in − I couldn't imagine anything bigger. I saw the whole pantomime, as my Brother had pictured it, mirrored in the confines of that shop.

There was the orchestra sitting in the narrow space behind the counter. It was the Salvation Army Band, the only orchestra I had encountered so far, and there they sat in their blue and scarlet uniforms blowing down their large brass trumpets and the drummer banging away like mad on his big drum. And there on the high counter came the two Misses Tyler, still dressed in black but, in honour of the occasion, wearing the Salvation Army Bonnets. They danced and they sang and they prinked. We sat in a row facing them on the cane-bottom chairs supplied for the customers, just the four of us, side by side, Father, Mother, Brother and me. It was all very hilarious and the Misses Tyler used all their professional charm; smiling down at me, tilting their heads, lifting their frocks at one side and kicking up their very thin black-stockinged legs. They did a good job. But I was not all that impressed. In fact, I looked forward to the pantomime with a certain amount of misgiving.

However, everyone else seemed to be working up an excitement so I endeavoured to enthuse too.

On the day, after an early lunch, we set off into the murk and made our way to the Lyric Theatre at Hammersmith. This was long before the days of people forming themselves into an orderly queue, and when we arrived we very quickly found ourselves being hustled in the middle of what I can only describe as a disorderly brawl. Mother grabbed both our hands, and Father hung on to Mother. We were pushed this way and that, until we had no breath left in our bodies. But everyone seemed good tempered. Nobody minded, it was all part of the afternoon's entertainment. A man played a violin, and another one sang to us. They passed a little box over the heads of the milling crowd and one or two people put the odd ha'penny in. It was all very singular. But very enjoyable.

All at once the doors were flung open and a man shouted out "Early doors this way".

We all heaved forward and made for the long-winding stone steps. There seemed to be hundreds of them. Mother was puffed and holding her heart when, at length, we reached the top. But once inside all frustrations were forgotten. The sight that met my eyes amazed me. It was oh so different from Miss Tyler's shop. We didn't sit on cane-bottom chairs. They were more like wooden forms. And the smell was not of moth balls and vinegar, but a very strong mixture of oranges and peppermints.

We were very high up indeed. Mother whispered, "We're in the upper circle". Some years after I knew it to be affectionately known as "The Gods".

And down below, miles away it seemed, in another world, was the orchestra pit which my Brother had described with such exactitude. Behind it was the stage itself, hidden at present by a huge red plush curtain. Then Father whipped out his Marcella cigar and lit it up. Every Christmas Mother gave him a Marcella cigar for a present. He either smoked it on Christmas day or saved it for a special occasion. This was it; and he lit it with a wax vesta (a box of which was a present to him from Brother Fred).

There we sat, in this paradise of a place, with the pungent smell of Father's cigar mingling with the smell of sweaty bodies. Father suddenly went all extravagant and bought a programme. Cost him a whole penny. Mother reprimanded him with "Daddy dear!".

"The pantomime is called Red Riding Hood", I heard him say, "hope young'n won't be frightened of the wolf!" I assured him that I liked 'wolfs'. I would have liked anything in this wondrous world.

I gazed down dizzily across the vast expanse. Yes, just as my Brother had so aptly depicted it. The angels on the walls, standing out in sharp relief, looking a bit stark in their plaster and gilt paint, and lo! What was this? The orchestra filing in, dressed not in Salvation Army uniform, but in neat black suits which Father referred to as 'evening dress'. All so different from what I had imagined, and they didn't blow violently down noisy brass trumpets, they wooed us tenderly on violins, and things called woodwinds. It all sounded very ethereal, so soothing, so inspired. I was transported into a world of romanticism, and when the curtain went up I was positively intoxicated. The kaleidescope of colour, the beautiful girls, the enchanting fairies – not a bit like the Misses Tyler in their black clothes and their high-button boots. It was fairyland, and the people in it were all celestials. Beings from another world. I made up my mind there and then that as soon as I was old enough, I would go on the stage. I was certain I belonged down there. I floated right out over the heads of the audience in front of me and took my rightful place in this fantastic world. What's more, I remained in it for several days after.

The chief comedy was played by Johnny Scofield (who later had a son to carry on the family tradition) and he sang a song which was new and bang up to date called "Won't you come home Bill Baily". Later he belted out another new song in which we all joined lustily – "Down by the old Bull and Bush". "He's enough to make a cat laugh", mused my Mother. I adored him. The only time I stopped laughing was when he had his bottom smacked in the School Scene. I had a little weep then, but nobody saw me, so it didn't count.

The title role was played by a winsome little thing whose name I believe was Edna May. I fell head over heels in love with her. And when she sang her song "Goodbye my little Usan", my heart swelled up and had I been able to get at her I would have proposed on the spot. For a great many weeks after that I would chase up the street after any small girl dressed in a Red Hood (they were very fashionable at the time) in the hope that it was my Little Red Riding Hood. I felt certain one day I would unearth her. But, of course, I never did, though from time to time I would pretend to write her a letter. I had been given one of those miniature stationery sets at Christmas and I got through the lot, filling the pages with scrawl, but which deep in my soul contained the tenderest words of love.

People are apt to think small children know nothing of the pangs of romance, but they are wrong. In my case, at any rate, it took a long time to wear off.

3

Holiday at the seaside

One day a letter arrived from my Aunt Jess. She lived at Leigh-on-Sea. She was the owner of a nice little shop that sold sweets and tobacco and odd bits of stationery. She was a business woman to her finger tips and as hard as nails. She said in the letter, she was so sorry to hear that little Vernon had been ill, and she thought a nice month at the seaside would do him good. She suggested coming up to London to collect my Brother and myself and taking us both back with her to Leigh-on-Sea.

I was in the seventh heaven. I couldn't remember my Aunt Jess, but if she was anything like my Aunt Maud, my holiday would be a howling success. And, to a certain extent it was. She would pick us up, she said, at Fenchurch Street Station. So Mother set off with us one dark winter's night and we all congregated in the restaurant at the Station. Aunt Jess bought us each a cup of tea, and she and Mother talked at length about past times and how good it was of her to give us boys a lovely holiday at the seaside, which wouldn't cost Mother a penny. Father, Mother told her, was fed up with his

job at Lovibonds and would Aunt Jess please look out for a
nice little empty shop at Leigh that Father could open up
and run and make some money like Aunt Jess had done.
Then, said Mother, smiling bravely at my Brother and I, we
would all be together at the seaside. She tried hard not to
show emotion as the train began to move away from the
platform, away from her two boys who meant more to her
than life itself, and Aunt Jess now stuck her great frame in
front of the window waving goodbye, which prevented us
getting a last glimpse of Mother.

I watched the bright metal advertisements sliding by as the
train gathered speed. In the dim gaslight they reflected their
message to mankind — Zam-Buk, rub it in; Keetings, for lice
and vermin; Beechams Pills, keep you fit. Aunt Jess pulled up
the window and said, "Your Mother's laughing her head off,
I've never seen her look so happy".

The train plunged into a dark tunnel, and I can still smell
the sickly stench of smoke that oozed through the cracks and
crevices. Trains in those days were particularly smelly; a
curious smell, hard to describe, but very pungent, and in no
time at all I was suffering from a bilious headache. My
Brother chatted away brightly to Aunt Jess, but I became
introvertive. For the first time I began to have qualms about
my immediate future.

I must have dropped off to sleep quite soon. I was
awakened shortly after, or so it seemed to me, to cries of,
"Here we are!" "Wake up sleepy head", and the thunder of
banging doors and yelling porters. In those days train doors
were not automatic, the porter's job was to bang them tight
shut and give a quick deft twist to the handle.

I followed my Aunt and Brother out of the station and
into the road. It was dark and very cold. I hung on tightly to
my brown-paper parcel that contained my change of clothes
and a few necessary accessories. It must have been nearly
midnight. I had never been up so late before. The shop was
only a short distance; my Aunt unlocked the shop door and
in we went.

She struck a match and lit the gas jet. We found ourselves

in the small parlour which led off from the shop. This tiny region served as sitting room, dining room and storage. It was, in fact, the only room downstairs with the exception of a gloomy old wash-house comprising a stone sink and a cement floor. A tin bath hung perilously on the wall.

"Go in there and wash your hands", commanded Aunt Jess, "and don't make a noise when you go upstairs, the girls are up there asleep".

She had two daughters, in age comparable to ourselves, whose names were Sybil and Freda. They led a rather Spartan life, we were soon to discover, and my Aunt was an enforcer of the strictest discipline. She believed whole heartedly in the maxim 'spare the rod and spoil the child'. She kept an old hairbrush handy, the bristles of which had fallen out long ago, and this was known in her household as the "poe-img smacker". On the slightest provocation she would whisk one of her daughters off her feet, fling her across her knee and leather into her small behind with this vicious weapon. Even her eldest daughter was not immune against this indignity, and on one such occasion I well remember the poor little soul crying out, "It's not so much the pain as the disgrace". But all this, as far as I was concerned, was in the future. My immediate desire was to get to bed, for I was oh, so tired.

Aunt Jess made us a glass of hot raspberry-flavoured stuff which I couldn't drink, and then we ascended the narrow staircase to our bedroom. By the dim light of the candle I could just make out the silhouettes of our two cousins, fast asleep in another bed. We undressed quickly and hopped in, snuggling up tight to each other for warmth, and soon fell asleep.

On the morrow we were awakened early by the two girls who had previously been instructed to give us each a welcoming kiss, which they did in a perfunctory sort of manner, Aunt Jess watching the proceedings from the doorway, candle in hand.

"Get washed and then come and have your breakfast", she ordered, "Girls first, boys wait outside till ready".

We, of course, washed at the sink in the wash-house and

21

were glad to get into the warmth of the parlour where a nice fire was crackling away up the chimney. Our breakfast consisted of porridge, which we didn't like and usually never had (especially with salt instead of sugar), and a cup of very strong tea. But, I told myself, it was holiday time and the good things were yet to come.

"Get your overcoats on boys", said Aunt Jess, "The girls are waiting to go".

"Oh good", replied my Brother, "Where are we going?"

"To school of course" said Aunt Jess.

And that was how I started my schooldays. The holiday to which we had so looked forward was to be spent five days a week at school.

I remember the old school well. It nestled at the bottom of Leigh Hill, quite close to my Aunt's shop. It was the typical "little red school house", except that this one had gone a bit green with ozone. It consisted of two class rooms, one for the infants and juniors, the other for the bigger pupils. Here I learned to write in a sanded box with a sharp stick. Three letter words had to be copied off the blackboard. When sufficiently proficient one was allowed a pencil and a copy book.

The lady teacher was very kind.

"How old are you?" she asked me on my arrival.

"Five", I lied remembering how Aunt Jess had primed me.

"You're small for five", she said dubiously, "however, if that's what you say".

"He is five, really", supported Sybil and Freda, according to instructions; and as free education for children of five and upwards was now a compulsory obligation, she had no alternative but to take me on.

I enjoyed school, once I'd got over the initial shock. The teacher allowed me to sit near the big fire in the centre of the classroom, and on very cold mornings we took "winter warmers" to school. These were small round tins (usually cocoa tins) in which we bored a few holes and then filled the tin with live coals. The poorer children would use smouldering rags (which stank the place out), but it kept our fingers warm and that was the main thing.

I liked the comradeship of school life. The older children, and especially the girls, were kindly disposed towards me, and I soon became adept at doing the innocent little boy stuff. I was fond of my teacher too; she was a gentle soul and very patient, but in the opposing classroom, I could continuously hear the swish of the cane being used on the older kids, and my sympathies went out to my Brother and Cousin Sybil.

We chanted the scriptures in low monotone, we chanted the multiplication table, we chanted from the history books, we chanted from the geography books, and at the end of the day we sang a hymn. I liked the hymn, it had a pretty tune. "Now the day is over", we sang and for some reason I always felt sad.

I soon acquired a taste for the arts, and learnt my tonic sol-fa. I was particularly interested in the vagaries of English History, but I muddled it a bit with Ancient History. Once, when called upon unexpectedly to give an answer as to what I would like to be when grown up, I replied unhesitatingly, "A King". A titter ran round the classroom. But my teacher kept a perfectly straight face.

"What would you do", she asked, "to prove yourself a king?"

And I said, "Were there to be a famine I would go out into the wilderness with buckets and buckets of water which I would personally pour over the land until it again became futile".

At weekends we were allowed to visit the seashore and do some paddling. Cold as it was, we used to slip out of our shoes and stockings and wade in. It was paralysing, but very invigorating. First time I went in I lost my nice new pair of boots. I left them on the harbour wall and when we came out of the water they had disappeared. My Aunt Jess was furious, she had to buy me another pair, and from then on I did as the other boys did when having a paddle, I tied them round my neck by the laces so that they dangled about in front of me.

Brother Fred was allowed on occasions to serve in the shop. He loved that and would sometimes be given a jujube for his services. He also found out about one or two things which were supposed to be exceedingly hush-hush. As, for instance, a nice large jujube stuck on to and under the base of the scales, which induced quite some deficiency of weight and made a considerable saving spread over a period.

My Aunt was also in a wax about some chocolate elephants she'd ordered for the last Christmas period and which, for some reason, had not turned out a good selling line.

"Get rid of the damned things, Fred", she coaxed my Brother, "They sell at a penny a time, but if we can't shift 'em, I'll knock 'em down to a ha'penny"

But to no avail. The customers wouldn't buy.

Then something happened that gave my Aunt Jess an idea. In those days the only popular cigarettes were Players and Goldflake, with Richmond Gem (done up in oval-shaped wrappers) and Woodbines (done up in open topped packets of five) to be had in the larger shops. One day a new consignment of Goldflake came in and, for the first time, inside the packet was a wrapping of silver paper. It was a new idea and very revolutionary. My Aunt mused about it in thoughtful vein for a long time.

"What a waste", she kept saying to my Brother, "Who needs cigarettes wrapped in silver paper". And then the idea dawned. "I know what we'll do, Fred," she said, "We'll take the bits of silver paper out of the fag packets and make nice little silver coats for the chocolate elephants."

Not only did she do just that, but she also upped the price to two pence. And the amazing part is they sold — every one of them.

My Father hated her. I remember once, for no particular reason, he plonked the teacosy on his head and said, "Mate, she's a rotter". But there was no denying the fact that she was a good business woman.

When our month's stay was nearly up my Brother and I could hardly wait for Mother's arrival. To say that we were

24

home-sick would be putting it mildly. We wanted to meet the train in, but Aunt said she didn't hold with boys hanging about railway stations. "Just as likely to stray on to the line and get run over", she said. "She's due to arrive sometime tomorrow afternoon, so if you hang about outside the shop you'll see her coming".

That night, the eve of Mother's arrival, we got so excited we were unable to eat our tea, and we found we couldn't concentrate on anything much either. So my Aunt Jess thought up a scheme which she said would tranquillise our disordered minds.

"I'll give a prize", she said, "to the first one I can make cry".

She then took each of us in turn, including her own two daughters, and she told us of some terrible fate which would shortly befall us.

She left me till last.

"Oh Vernon", she said casually, "I forgot to tell you, your Mother will not be coming tomorrow after all".

I won the prize easily.

4

The Dudderies

Aunt Jess organised the whole thing from beginning to end. It was to be a confectioners and restaurant combined. It was to belong to us entirely, but Aunt Jess supplied the stock to start us off, on the understanding that Father paid her back so much every week — with a little interest for herself — until the debt was finally settled.

The shop was located in Westcliff, about two miles distant from Aunt Jess's shop at Leigh. It was just off the main road, and trams passed the door.

"You can't go wrong, mate", said Jess, "with summer coming on, it'll be a goldmine". She dressed the window, very attractively, for which she pointed out she was giving her services "gratis and free of charge". She also arranged the shelves and priced everything. All we had to do was get the customers in and relieve them of their money.

It sounded marvellous. We were in the seventh heaven. Father bought up some second hand tables and chairs at a sale and they were nicely arranged in the spacious shop.

"You can't go wrong", Aunt Jess kept saying, licking her

fingers clean as she arranged the sticky sweets along the counter. She pointed out that she had started off some friends of hers in the same way. They had a little shop round the corner from us which they proudly called "San Toy". They had been in it about two weeks. We got to know them very well in due course. A husband and wife by the name of West, and they had a sylph-like daughter called Mabel, aged midway between my Brother and myself. Mrs. West was a woman of refinement, with very high principles. She lacked a sense of humour albeit, and could, I suppose, have been described as "straight-laced". Frankie West was a highly popular man, a gentleman to his finger tips or, as we said in those days, "a bit of a la-di-dah!" He had a long flowing moustache and a long flow of fascinating phraseology to go with it. He was a great success with the ladies. They adored him. He was so polite and considerate. Altogether a charming man. The only thing against him was his unfortunate lack of luck. Everything he touched went wrong. But he would always somehow La-di-dah his way out of it, and before you could say Jack Robinson, he was up to some other lark. Usually something dubious and not too laborious. But everyone loved him, with perhaps the exception of his wife, who on occasions failed to see his funny side. For all that, they were a devoted couple and we struck up a friendship with them that was to be almost life-long. For many years we treasured a photograph of Mrs. West and Mabel, taken about the time we first knew them. Mabel, in a pretty white summer frock, with Mrs. West's hands placed just underneath it, so that they didn't show in the photograph, because she bit her nails.

We named our restaurant "The Sunbeam", after Mother's favourite hymn, "Jesus wants me for a sunbeam". We had an arrangement with the butcher next door to supply us on the dot with meat in accordance with a customer's wish. Mother would pop in through the backway, he would serve her with whatever was required, Mother would pop back into her kitchen, cook it and serve it, and when the customer had gone she would nip back with the cash.

As a small boy, I was more interested in the confectionery side. Thanks to Aunt Jess we started off with quite a good selection. There was nothing like the variety of sweets then as we have to-day, and many of them were quite different. I remember them all, so well! Sherbert Suckers. These consisted of small paper bags of sherbert, fastened at the top with a small liquorice tube through which you sucked up your sherbert. We had Sherbert Dabs too, which were similar, but instead of a liquorice tube there was inserted a piece of toffee on a stick. You dabbed the toffee in the sherbert and sucked it dry, demolishing the toffee dab afterwards of course. These cost a ha'penny each. Then we had liquorice strips and liquorice ladders for a farthing. Another popular line was a sweet shaped like a small bird's egg. These were sold for a penny a quarter. The fascination here was that as you sucked them they continually changed colour. A great success with young boys who enjoyed taking them out of their mouths every now and then to show the change of colour to anyone who might be interested. Toffee came in shallow tins and was broken up with a small hammer. Wrapped toffee had not been invented. There were two makes only that I can remember. Sharps Creamy and Mackintoshes. Both were delicious, particularly the latter. It formed a residue on the outside which tasted faintly of salt. The toffee, when broken up, was put straight into a paper bag and the only snag was it soon became sticky.

We stocked the accepted brands of cigarettes of the period, Goldflake, Players and Woodbines, done up in packets of five; and Father also kept a stock of St. Julian tobacco for pipe smokers, because that happened to be the brand he smoked himself.

The only known mineral waters of the day were Lemonade and Ginger Beer. Father ordered in a crate of each. Stone's Ginger Beer, as it was called, was an exquisite drink. It came in stone bottles, and there was a delightful pop when you opened it. When poured out there was a lovely substantial froth on the top, and the flavour was quite different from the ginger beer of to-day. Minerals could be poured out and drunk on the premises or taken away as desired. Mother got in a large tin of real coffee, and an extra packet of tea. Also a tin of sherbert, so that small boys and girls could have a glass for a ha'penny, if they couldn't afford lemonade or ginger beer at a penny.

It all sounded very feasible, and it's difficult to know what went wrong. We were on a semi-main road with trams passing all day and most of the night. It didn't help, of course, when the Council decided to have the road taken up and new drains put down almost immediately after we moved in. The smell was pretty ghastly, and even turned us off our own meals, let alone prospective customers. We did, however, do a fair trade in teas and coffees with the men who were working on the site. Aunt Jess came along one morning to collect her dibs and was furious with Mother because she was serving real coffee.

"You'll never make money like that, gal", she said, "make it from that bottled stuff, and then sprinkle a few coffee pips on top when you serve it, they'll never know the difference".

Mother was appalled, but Jess slipped up the road, bought a bottle of Camp Coffee and served the next customer herself. It happened to be a Corporation Official, rotund and somewhat pompous. He sniffed the coffee apprehensively, then took a sip and gave an encouraging smile.

"Now, that's what I call a *real* cup of coffee", he said, "when you can see the coffee grains floating about on the top". And he congratulated Aunt Jess and thanked her.

Spring gave way to summer and the weather turned sizzling hot. Aunt Jess said, "Now is the time to make a lot of money making ice cream". In those days people only ate ice cream when the weather was hot, it was not universally eaten as it is to-day, so the thing was to get in quick while the warm weather lasted. Aunt Jess loaned us an ice cream barrel; when I say "loaned", I should, of course, say "rented". It all went on the weekly bill with the stock she had provided earlier, and for which Father was trying his damdest to pay back. All ice cream was made by hand then. The ice cream powder was put into a metal container with milk and water, and on the outside of the container, between that and the barrel, were solid lumps of ice which one bought each morning from the ice-van which called round. You broke the ice up into small particles, wedged it in, and then turned a handle which rotated the canister. It might take half an hour or more before the ice cream was set and ready for consumption. By that time it was quite likely the weather had worsened and nobody wanted it, in which case it melted away and you lost the lot. It was tremendously hard work making the stuff. Sometimes Mother would give a hand turning the handle, while Father would drop into a chair until he got back enough strength to carry on again.

Meantime, our friendship with the Wests ripened, for they weren't doing very well either.

"How are things with you?" my Father would ask, and Frankie West would reply, "Terrible! We took three ha'pence yesterday, and four-pence the day before".

On occasions Mabel would come dashing into our shop asking for a packet of cigarettes pronto. It would transpire that a customer of their's had asked for a certain brand of cigarettes which Frankie hadn't got (it was probably doubtful if he'd got any brand at all, to be candid), whereupon the customer would be told a new consignment had just arrived, and would he mind waiting whilst the crate was being opened up. Frankie would then disappear into the back parlour, making a lot of noise with a hammer until Mabel returned via the back entrance with the cigarettes, which would be handed to the customer with a smile and apologies for the delay. Mabel would then return to us with the money.

"Never disappoint a customer", Frankie would say with his charming smile.

Brother Fred's school broke up for the customary summer holiday. One month only in those days. He was allowed sometimes to serve in the shop, having had some experience with Aunt Jess at Leigh. Other times we took ourselves off to the sea front, collecting seashells, paddling and building sand castles.

We tired of this after a bit, and my Brother said, "I know

what. We'll take a trip to Leigh-on-Sea and look up some of our pals".

So we walked to Leigh, children thought nothing of walking a couple of miles or so, and we called in on my Aunt Jess to see if we could play with Sybil and Freda. But meanwhile Aunt Jess had decided that Sybil should learn the violin. She was made to attend evening class at school once a week where, with a lot of others, she was put through the techniques of this delicate instrument. She was made to practise four hours a day, and as she had various household chores to execute in between, poor little soul had very little spare time for going out to play. When Aunt Jess was asked if she didn't think it was rather hard on a small girl of nine years she replied with a touch of sadistic glee, "Her tears run down the bow, mate, and drop off the end".

So that ruled Sybil and Freda out. But we dug up some of the lads we had met at the little school in Leigh, and we re-visited our old haunts. There was a little humped bridge close to the railway station which one had to negotiate to reach the small harbour, and one of our favourite games was to wait for an on-coming train and drop bits of wood down the funnel as it passed underneath. You got a point if you scored a bulls eye, and it wasn't as easy as it might sound. Most times the train had just pulled up at the station, so that, although it passed by quite slowly, it was belching great clouds of black smoke in its endeavour to get going. Your aim was mostly guesswork. You estimated the drop in advance and then hopped quickly out of the smoke as the train approached. More often than not, arguments would ensue as to whether you had actually scored, because the other lads looking on would have their vision impaired by the smoke too.

"You missed it", my Brother would say with streaming eyes.

"No I never", I would declare, and then the adjudicators would be appealed to, and they didn't know half the time, either.

It was an exciting game that challenged our endurance and

kept us on our toes. One day, however, my Brother, in a particularly ambitious mood, was seen mounting the steps with a large half brick at the ready. From then on the station master himself took a hand in the game, and we had to run for our lives.

It was in the High Street at Leigh-on-Sea that I witnessed my first fire. A "house on fire" held a certain magic for people in those days. A fire engine would be followed by an excited crowd, sometimes for miles. There were fire-alarms dotted about the main thoroughfares that looked not unlike miniature pillar boxes. Bright red in colour, with a rounded apex in which was inserted a small piece of glass. Inside, in bold letters, it said IN CASE OF FIRE BREAK GLASS AND PULL BELL. Presumably the alarm-bell was connected directly with the fire station.

Quietly to myself, I always harboured a desire to break the glass and pull the toggle, just to see what happened. But one Sunday afternoon we could hardly believe our eyes when a man actually dashed up and did it.

We waited with bated breath, as a small crowd quickly gathered. It seemed quite a long time, as it always does, when you are waiting for something desperate to happen. Then we saw it coming in the distance. A never-to-be-forgotten sight. The bright red fire engine with the huge brass chimney smoking away in the rear. The sleek well-trained horses galloping towards us, and the firemen in their brightly-polished helmets clinging on for dear life and shouting, "Hi, hi, hi!" plus the clang of the enormous brass bell. It was enough to wake the dead. A soul-stirring drama guaranteed to shake up the liver of any homo sapien.

"Where's the fire?" the head fireman called out.

"Maypole dairy, in the main street", shouted back the man. And off we all went, hell for leather. I had never run so fast in my life. I felt my legs buckling under me.

"The Maypole" was more than just a dairy. It could be compared with our modern Express Dairy. It was a very popular store and noted for its high-quality butter. This was always stacked in huge slabs on the counter. The assistant shaped it to the size required with a small pair of dabs, like little shovels. Finally he gave it a slap with another one on which was the imprint of a cow, and this was the Maypole trade mark.

Being Sunday the shop was closed. But the fire was not actually inside the shop — it appeared to be in the upper regions, and smoke was pouring out of the roof. The firemen seemed to be at a loss to know what to do. They broke down the front door of the shop, but apparently, once inside, they found all was bolted and barred against them. How to get to the upper part of the building? That was the question. They held a hurried consultation. The Chief then decided to send a man up the ladder to inspect the roof. The ladder was a rather elementary affair, slotted together in three pieces. However, they got it up against the front of the building at last, and we waited expectantly as one of the firemen ascended it in his large heavy boots.

He disappeared over the top and was lost to view for quite some little while. Then suddenly he reappeared; we could see his face and his bright golden helmet silhouetted by what was now an enormous cloud of black smoke.

"Oi can't see no fire up 'ere", he called out in his rich Essex dialect. And he got a laugh from the crowd, the size of which any Music Hall comedian would have been proud of.

Most of the local firemen were on a voluntary basis and had other jobs. Their fireman's uniform was kept at home. Should a fire be reported, a maroon was fired, the respective firemen would dash off home, get into their uniform and hurry to the fire station as quickly as possible.

A friend of my Father's told a tale, the veracity of which I cannot vouch for, but he swore it was true. It was to the effect that one of the local firemen, who happened to be his personal friend, once had a very embarrassing experience. He lived in a fair-sized house which boasted a long back garden, and attached to the garden was a nice little allotment which he rented annually from the Council. One day, whilst tending his crops with love and care, he heard the maroon go off with its customary big bang. He downed tools, hurried out of his allotment, through the long garden, up the rear stairs and into his back bedroom where his fire gear was kept. He jumped into his fireman's jacket and helmet, but couldn't find his uniform trousers. He hunted high and low, but they were nowhere to be seen. (It subsequently transpired that they were in the bed, being pressed between the mattress. A customary habit in those days, the object being to put a nice crease in them. But he had, on the spur of the moment, forgotten that he'd placed them there, following the last fire).

His agitation knew no bounds when he distinctly heard the clang of the fire engine bell in the distance, for he realised they had departed without him. In sheer desperation, he opened the wardrobe and pulled on the first pair of trousers that came to hand. They happened to be a pair which belonged to his fourteen year old son, and the fit was not noticeably good.

He tore down the back stairs, up the long garden path, and away through the allotment; for this was a short cut to the fire station. On arrival he enquired breathlessly as to the location of the fire and was told it was at his own house – in the front parlour.

Meantime, back at the shop, things were not panning out too well. Frankie West would look in sometimes and say in his la-di-dah manner, "Hallo Rowley old boy. How's trade?"

And Father would reply, "What trade? I haven't seen any".

Then Frankie would drop his voice and say, "Well, as a matter of fact, old man, I've only popped out for a while because it's Jessy's morning to collect her percentage of the week's takings".

"Good God", Father would reply, "She'll be along *here* any minute. Let's go and have a drink." And off they'd go to drown their sorrows.

It was round about this time that "The Sunbeam" and the "San Toy" were re-christened "The Dudderies". Frankie came in one morning looking a little morose, which was rather odd for him. He adjusted his pince nez with both hands and looked my Father straight in the eye.

"It's no good pretending, Rowley old boy, and it's no good beating about the bush. My shop is a dud!" And he looked at my Father as though he was going to be truly amazed at this great discovery.

"If you call your's a dud", said Father, "What the hell do you call mine?" Frankie considered for a moment and then said,

"A duddier dud!"

And being gifted with the extraordinary sense of humour that people seemed to have in those days, they both roared with laughter. So from then on, in our own private circle of friends, the shops were affectionately known as "The Dudderies". The only one who failed to see the funny side of it was Aunt Jess, who said she was getting through a small fortune in tram fares, coming over for her rake-off and going back every time empty handed.

There was a lot of nice open country on the outskirts of Westcliff and a number of orchards that teemed with apple trees and other delectable fruit. We boys spent a lot of our time that summer scrumping (for the un-enlightened, that means climbing up trees and pinching apples that don't, by law, belong to you). One day we arrived back home choc-a-bloc with vicious-looking green apples. We had got armfuls of them. In our pockets, stuffed up our jackets, down our trousers, every conceivable place.

"Look Mum", said Brother Fred, as we poured our ill-gotten gains out on the kitchen table. "We thought you could sell them in the shop. That ought to help".

"All profit", I piped in.

"Don't be silly, snapped back Mother, turning the wretched-looking things over with her index finger. "Who do you think would want to buy soured little crab-apples?"

There was a pause.

"Cover them with sugar", I suggested after a bit. Mother gave a little start.

"Son", she murmured, "You've given me an idea. I'll heat up that Sharps Creamy toffee which we can't sell, and cover the apples with it".

"Toffee apples!" cried Brother Fred, who remembered having had some once at a fair. Nobody had thought of the idea round our way.

"Toffee apples!" repeated Mother, with a dramatic gesture. She was inclined always to be a little theatrical in times of stress. Brother Fred, who had recently started carpentry lessons at school, got busy with a penknife and some sticks of firewood, and soon shaped a few dinky little strips of wood to stick in each apple in the accepted way.

From a sales point of view, they were a furore. If you will excuse the simile, they went like "hot cakes". Mother retailed them at a penny each. Trouble was, they were not symmetrical in size. So the bigguns went first. In fact, as the day grew longer, the apples grew smaller, and there was a deal of comparing sizes outside the shop door.

One man came in with his howling kid and threatened to punch Father's head if he didn't give him a bigger apple. Which surprised Father because he'd only just come in and didn't know what it was all about.

"I do believe our luck is on the turn", avowed Mother, ever hopeful. "All we want now is some hot weather, and the same clientele will automatically come to us for ice creams".

Even at that age, I smiled to myself at Mother's reference to our customers being a "clientele". If you could have seen some of them you would know what I mean. But the hot weather was reluctant to come. It was a typical English summer. The sun would peep through almost apologetically, and then pop back again.

"It's a licker", said Mother, "No sooner your Father gets the ice cream ready and down it pours cats and dogs". There were of course no weather forecasts in those days, so it was a hit and miss affair all the way. But one morning it really looked hopeful. Father got busy with the ice cream machine immediately, and we all went to the shop door in turns, watching the sun having a game of cat and mouse.

"A watched pot never boils" quoted Mother when it got near lunch time. "Tell you what ducky, you take the two boys for a nice walk, you're looking very peaky lately, and I'll look after the shop".

"Yes", admitted Father. "I am feeling a bit dicky, perhaps a bit of fresh air along the front will put me right".

So Father blew the dust off his straw boater and off we went. We took a long walk into Southend-on-Sea. I used to love Southend, and at this time of the year it was full of cockneys on holiday from London's East End. All ripe for fun and laughter. I loved the smell of the cockle stalls too. Everywhere was so busy. We passed the Jolly Boys concert party on the beach, and then we had a look at Finlay Dunns which was under a large canvas awning and was a rather more refined type of summer entertainment. It was still quite chilly, but the clouds suddenly broke and a reluctant sun peeped through. We passed two women dressed in sombre black. Heavy serge overcoats down to their ankles and droopy black hats, one with feathers. As we passed we heard one of them say, "Coo, ain't it bloody hot". The other wiping her forehead with the back of her hand, replied, "Yes, what we need now is a nice cool shower of rain".

Further on we came across two little girls wearing quite the largest sun hats I've ever seen in my life. They were the size of cartwheels, made of straw and threaded with pink ribbon. Indeed, their hats were so gigantic that to allow us to pass it became necessary for the smaller one to whip hers off her head and allow it to trail behind her on the ground. The older girl, noticing this, gave her arm a good slap and said,

"Put your straw r'at on, you silly cow, or you'll get sunstroke".

With that the sun withdrew hastily behind a cloud and all was back to normal.

Suddenly Father went mad. He said, "What about a nice tram ride home?"

"Oh daddy, yes please, please!" I yelled. I loved the trams at Southend. They were quite different from the trams in the London suburbs. There was more of a friendliness about them. They were open-topped, and operated on the overhead-wire system. We boys, of course, always went on top, there was so much to see, and however often we went on one it was always an adventure. The tram used to make a fascinating high note every time it rounded a corner. Shrill and sustained, rather like a passé soprano slightly off-key.

My Brother was cautious. "Dad", he said, "Do you think you should? It'll cost you fourpence from here. Tuppence for you, penny each for us".

"Ah, to hell with it", said Father, "I've got a feeling our luck's about to change. Let's hurry back to Mother and see how many ice creams she's sold".

We alighted from the tram right outside our shop door and we could hardly believe our eyes. The well-dressed window was completely empty. We entered the shop and that was devoid of stock too. We sauntered into the back parlour as in a dream. Mother was on her knees washing her hair in a basin. She pulled her hair to one side as we entered and addressed Father with one eye shut.

"Jess has been here", she said, "She's foreclosed".

"Foreclosed?" uttered Father.

"Yes. She arrived in a cab with two suitcases and she's taken the lot. She said it belonged to her anyway".

"Did you sell any ice cream?" asked Father, which sounds silly in retrospect, but it was the only thing he could think of.

"No", said Mother, rinsing her hair and holding her head low over the basin, "She took that too, ice cream in it and all".

There was a lull in the conversation, and Mother started drying her hair.

"Don't worry ducky", she said brightly, "I'll make a nice strong cup of tea. Something will turn up".

5

Village of Hounslow

Father got a job at Hounslow, so we moved there. In those far-off days Hounslow was little more than a country village. The house we moved into was brand new. It boasted an indoor lavatory. The word "toilet" had not so far come into popular use. Refined people called it "the lavatory", and the others called it the "closet". My Father was wont to call anyone he didn't like "a closet" too, but that's another matter. Mother was all against indoor sanitation. She considered it unhygienic.

"Things of that description", she said, with a touch of hauteur, "should be built outside the house, and the further away the better".

It was a nice little house, Jerry-built no doubt, but compact. It smelt of new paint and varnish and, mixed with it, was a suggestion of escaping gas. But it was bright and gay. I loved it. Mother was dubious and Father said we would have to take in a lodger to help us pay the rent.

So we let the middle room downstairs to an elderly lady who moved in the following week. She professed to be of pious habits, religious and unmarried.

"I have plighted my troth with the Lord God", she would say to Mother as she followed her about, and would then add, "Excuse me, my dear. I must go to my room and read a chapter from the Bible". In fact, whenever an awkward situation arose, such as being asked to pay her rent (which she never did), she would excuse herself and say in a sanctimonious voice, "I must go to my room and read a chapter".

However, one day, while the old lady was out, Mother took advantage of the situation and peeped into her room. She had difficulty in opening the door for gin bottles, and it was quickly borne in upon Mother that the old lady drank. As Father said, "Reading a chapter" was a crafty euphemism for "having a noggin".

She was asked to find other accommodation as soon as convenient, but when, on the next evening, she followed Father up the road, singing and dancing and suggesting that his parents were never married, she was told to get out there and then, at once!

"Trouble is", said Mother, "the rent of this house is so high (four shillings a week) we must either let part of it, or I must get a job".

Father laughed his head off. Women in those days did not go out to work, especially married ones.

Mother said, "I don't care a tinker's cuss, I'm going to earn some money, so there!" And she began to think out what talents she had that might be commercialised.

"I know", she said all of a sudden, "I'm quite good at making my own clothes, I could advertise myself privately as a dressmaker".

Her idea of advertising privately was to put a postcard in our sitting room window which said, in Mother's best hand, DRESSMAKING DONE HERE. Sure enough (and as if to silence the critics) two days later a lady called to discuss with Mother a new costume she was contemplating having made. She had bought the material, she told Mother, and would bring it along if Mother felt she was sufficiently competent to make it. They talked at considerable length, and the lady left, saying she would call the following afternoon with the stuff.

On the morrow, I unobtrusively watched Mother pottering about in the sitting room, peeping nervously through the half open blinds and nearly jumping out of her skin at every unexpected noise. Suddenly, she drew back, I was shushed violently and told to keep quiet. The lady had come. She knocked three times. But Mother just skulked in the shadows, and the lady took herself off again.

I overheard Mother discussing it with Father that night.

"I just couldn't face it, ducky", she said, "I'll have to think of something else".

Strange to say, providence itself came forward with an excellent idea. Mother had always been very psychic, and was extremely good at telling fortunes. She had quite a small reputation for it, in fact. One day, an old friend from Acton called to see her. She had brought another woman and wanted to know if Mother would be so obliging as to read her friend's hand.

"You remember what you told me when you read mine at Acton, my dear. It all came true, every word! And my friend is dying for you to tell her future too. She'll pay you, of course. What do you charge?"

Quick as lightening Mother said, "Sixpence for palmestry, shilling for the cards".

"I'd like both done", said the friend modestly, trying not to blush. And from then on Mother, by word of mouth, worked up a nice little clientele who paid sixpence a time to have their fortunes laid bare.

The small income she accumulated was spent mostly on things for the home. Father was keen on having a roll of the new Cork Lino that was being advertised extensively. He said it would look lovely in the hall and give it an air of gentility when Mother's ladies called to have their palms read. Mother agreed, and they chose a piece in pale green which stretched from the front door to the kitchen. Father spent a whole evening tacking it down, but for some unknown reason one little bit always stuck up. It was probably due to a knot in the floor board underneath, but whatever the cause, it had a devastating effect on Father, who never failed to trip over it. The extraordinary part about it was that nobody else did, just Father. And he always swore at it, and said he would get a hammer and nail one day and tack it down. But he never did.

I shall never forget the day when, in response to a rat-tat at the front door, Mother opened it and there stood the young parlour-maid who worked for Mrs. Rowlands, the wife of the politician at Acton.

"Remember what you told me last week when you read my hand?" she gasped.

"Yes, come in", replied Mother, quickly ushering her inside, for fortune telling was strictly illegal.

"Well", went on the young maid, "every word has come to pass. That chap is going to marry me after all".

"I'm so glad", said Mother, visualising another bright sixpence on the way.

"And now", continued the maid in a low whisper, "my missis wants you to read *her* hand".

"Not, not Mrs. Rowlands", spluttered Mother, "Oh no, I couldn't. She's a lady".

"Makes no difference, mam. Ladies and servants all in the same boat when it comes to their future. She's dead keen, and she wishes me to make an appointment for tomorrow night. She'll come in her carriage after dark. Of course, she'll pay more'n I pay. Charge her a shilling for her 'and, and two shillings for the cards. She wants to go the whole hog".

To say Mother was flabbergasted is to put it but mildly. Not only the money, but the realisation that a well-bred lady was to visit our house in person. Father, too, went all limp with excitement. He had enormous respect for Mrs. Rowlands, and we two boys, in the stupid way that boys have, were convinced that Dad was a bit sweet on her!

The whole thing was to be stage-managed to the smallest detail. Father would open the front door and bow Mrs. Rowlands in. Mother would be secreted behind the kitchen door until Mrs. Rowlands had been safely piloted up the hall and deposited in the sitting room. Mother would then make a star entrance, hand extended. Brother Fred would take care to keep out of the way, and I was to be put to bed.

The big night arrived. It was tense. Mrs. Rowlands' carriage drew up outside. There was a knock at the door. I crept out of bed and took up a listening position at the top of the stairs. I heard Father walk with sedate step and open the door. He bowed Mrs. Rowlands in with ceremony. He then made to open the sitting room door and, as usual, stumbled over the projecting bit of cork lino.

"Sod!" said Father, before he had time to think what he was doing, and then immediately began to apologise to Mrs. Rowlands for his bad language. Mother, too, forgot about her star entrance and raced up the hall saying, "Daddy, please!" Mrs. Rowlands said it was quite all right, not to worry at all.

"He never swears as a rule", pleaded Mother.

"I don't know what came over me", said Father meekly.

Mrs. Rowlands entered the sitting room and Mother followed and closed the door. Mrs. Rowlands had just got her hands stretched out, awaiting her worldly fate, when Father appeared at the door brandishing a hammer.

"I'm going to nail that lino down before we get any more accidents", he told Mrs. Rowlands, "Should have been done long ago. And again, please forgive me for my dreadful language".

Mrs. Rowlands assured him it was quite all right, and advised him to forget the whole incident.

"Oh no", persisted Father, "I'll nail it down right now, otherwise some lovely lady like yourself may come through that door and, before you can say knife, she'll trip arse over head".

So saying, he bowed himself out, closed the door very quietly and started on his noisy hammering.

We got to know quite a lot of nice people at Hounslow. I palled up with the local lamplighter. We had only one street lamp and it happened to be right outside our house. I used to wait for him at dusk, swinging on the front garden gate, and along he'd come with his long pole which he'd poke up the lamp and, with the hook attached, he would deftly turn on the switch that ignited the mantle. I used to watch his performance with fascination and he would always have a cheery word for me. He used to leave his bike at the end of the road because, being a brand new neighbourhood, the road was not yet made up and it consisted of deep cart tracks carved out of heavy clay which, on wet days, could be quite dangerous. I'd follow him to the end of the road and watch him take off, sitting very stiff with his pole standing straight up over his left shoulder. In the distance I would see him igniting other lamps, which he managed to do without even dismounting from his bike. He would often turn and wave to me from the dim distance, and then I would nip back up the road and indoors feeling life was pretty good.

On recommendation from the church, of which we were part of the congregation, my Brother and I joined the Band of Hope. The Band of Hope was a bastian against strong drink. One had to sign a pledge to be a total abstainer before being admitted as a member. We signed without hesitation, and told our Father so when we got home.

"We have sworn to be teetotallers for the whole of our lives", we said with divine conviction.

"Good", said Father, who liked his drop, and then I fancy I heard him say under his breath, "Wish there were more like you".

The Band of Hope indulged now and then in magic lantern shows, all of which epitomised great moral fibre, and on the way out we were always given a bun and orange. On one momentous occasion, in addition to the usual magic lantern show, we had a special thing provided called the Bioscope. We sat on the edge of our seats and marvelled at it. The pictures actually moved. One of them showed two men fighting with swords. Quite suddenly, one man was seen to be crawling along the ground with an agonised look on his face.

"He's wounded!" I heard someone say behind me. And there was a general gasp.

We went home in a daze. It was a Saturday night, and every Saturday night, whether we needed it or not, we were given a doze of liquorice powder to keep our bowels active. I hated the stuff, it tasted poisonous but, on this occasion, we were so entranced with what we had seen, we hardly noticed it. Sometimes Mother would relent and substitute brimstone and treacle for the dreaded liquorice powder, which had the same bodily effect but tasted less terrible.

It was roughly the following day I suppose that I crossed swords with Father, as I often did. I remember he gave me a good hard wallop and, in the accepted way, I was turned out of the room until I had repented. The door would be then opened and I would be invited back and expected to say, "Sorry Dad, I'll be a better boy in future". This may sound harsh treatment in these enlightened days, but it was fairly universal then and quite candidly I don't think it did any of us much harm.

Anyhow, on this occasion when the door was opened to me, I crawled in on my left side, slowly and dramatically. My parents stopped their conversation in mid-stream and stared at me in astonishment.

"Whatever's the matter with him", my Mother said with obvious concern.

I twisted my face upward and gazed at my Father with a doleful eye.

"You've wounded me", I said, and was completely taken by surprise at the laugh I got in response.

Life went on merrily at Hounslow. We had a long back garden which faced on to a semi-main road, and quite often the Lancers from a nearby barracks would march past, some mounted on beautiful sleek horses, and led by their band which invariably played the popular march called "Blaze Away". It used to thrill me to the marrow and Dobbin, my wooden horse, would be yanked up to the end of the garden to enjoy the spectacle too. The Lancers in their helmets with the tassel dangling at one side was, to me, an unforgettable sight, and the strident notes of the brass band filled me with wonder and stimulated my imagination. After they had passed by I would sit astride Dobbin and enact the scene over and over again.

Another deep impression during this period was my first visit to a Music Hall. I think, if memory serves me right, it was called the Chiswick Empire. At any rate, it was quite a journey, and Father had gone over that way for an interview concerning a new job. He never stayed anywhere long. So we went over with Mother and we all met in the foyer of the theatre.

One turn that impressed me very much was a comedian called Wilkie Bard. He did a sketch with two or three others, and each of them in turn would say to him, "Is your name Wilkie?" and he'd say, "Yes", and the other chap would say, "Well, you're Bard". And wherever he went they wouldn't let him in! The audience shrieked with laughter at this stock gag every time it was cracked, and I laughed louder and longer than the rest.

Every Monday morning Mother did her washing in the huge copper that was a part of the scullery. All houses boasted one of these. It was a main feature and considered pretty important. The copper was set in a huge mould of cement, and it was usually lined with zinc. The actual cavity was large, about two feet across. The water was heated from underneath by a small coal fire which was kept in place by an iron lattice-type door. Little bits of coal and smouldering cinders would tipple out and these were collected in a tray underneath supplied for the purpose.

Like most kids too young for school, I used to love helping Mother do the week's washing. With the Music Hall turns in mind, and Wilkie Bard in particular, I thought to add a little entertainment to the exigencies of washday. I would hold up a garment and say to it, "Is your name Wilkie?" and in a different voice reply, "Yes", and I would then say, "Right! Well, you're being bathed!" and in the water it went.

Mother never failed to laugh at this joke and told Father about it. It wasn't till I was much older I realised, thinking back, that I had got the gag wrong.

Still, it helped to relieve the tensions of Mother's labours, for there is no doubt that washing day was extremely hard going for women in those days. Few could afford to have a woman to help out and the luxury of sending clothes to the laundry was out of the question for all but the well-to-do. Swirling the clothes round in the copper then scrubbing them on what was called the drubbing-board, and putting them through the huge and cumbersome mangle must have been hard going for even the toughest female. In between all this, of course, she had to continually rake out the cinders and feed the small fire.

I always watched Mother with a calculating eye on washday. It was the only time she would lose patience and I might finish up with a boxed ear. And a swipe round the ear with a wet hand always seemed, for some reason, much worse than a dry clip. I don't know why. I suppose it's the small boy's natural aversion to water.

I spent my fifth birthday at Hounslow, which meant, of course, that we spent Christmas there too, as my birthday falls six days before. In the house right opposite us lived a family called the Kerslakes. They had two children, a boy called Joe, who was my Brother's age and a girl called Mary, who was my age. The Kerslakes were just that bit superior, and Joe went to a private school. He was, however, very friendly with my Brother, and they played together quite often, in a refined sort of way. Sometimes, he would visit our house and stay to tea. He always displayed marked decorum, and as my Brother was that way inclined too, their friendship ripened; they seemed to have so much in common.

Mother was delighted when we received an official invitation for Brother Fred to attend a Christmas party they were holding, but the invitation was worded in such a way that we didn't know whether I was included in it or not.

We watched from the front door as Brother Fred slipped away into the darkness, and we heard him knock on the door opposite. There was a flicker of light as the door was opened and we heard Mrs. Kerslake's voice.

"Where's your little Brother?"

I was up the stairs and into my best suit before Brother had time to negotiate the rough road on the way back. But my clothes were whipped off again pretty quick to enable

Mother to give me a good scrubbing before departing for the great adventure. Then, hand in hand with Brother Fred, we picked our way over the ruts in the road to Mrs. Kerslake's house, shivering with suppressed excitement and smelling faintly of Sunlight soap.

The Kerslake's were not wealthy people but they were "comfortable". Their house was larger and nicer than ours, and it was tastefully furnished with thick carpets on the floor. In the corner was a large Christmas tree with a variety of small gifts attached and on top was a doll dressed up to look like a fairy. A huge fire half up the chimney raised the temperature of the room to that lovely dreamy opulent kind of feeling, and there was a delightful smell of ladies' perfume and milk chocolate. I thought I had never seen a room look, or smell, so beautiful.

Joe and Mary were waiting for us. They stood up politely as we entered, and Mary immediately took me under her wing. She was an attractive little girl, with long corn-coloured hair and a fringe. Her cheeks were very red, probably the result of the hot fire, and she had twinkling blue eyes and a perfect rosebud mouth. I remember she wore a frilly white frock with a wide blue sash. She looked very pretty. I had never spoken to her before, but she was perfectly at ease, and my shyness quickly wore off.

We played all sorts of games, mostly Christmas presents of Joe's and Mary's, and then we were taken into the dining room and sat down to a really scrumptious meal. No other kids turned up, we were the only two who had been invited. I imagine the Kerslakes were fussy about the type of children their's mixed with. We were very much on our best behaviour. After the gratifying meal we went back to the room with the big fire and played more games in which Mr. and Mrs. Kerslake joined. I could never remember just when I dropped off, but I was awakened suddenly by Mother, who was wrapping me in an eiderdown.

"I'll get him to bed", I heard Mother saying in a voice that sounded a hundred miles away, "and Fred, you can stay just ten more minutes, no more".

Then there were a lot of "goodnights" and "thanks for having them", and I was taken home and put to bed. I was furious with myself. The most wonderful night of my life and I must needs go and drop off to sleep. "You chump, you silly chump", I kept saying over and over again. The thought of having missed some of that enchanting evening was more than I could bare.

I felt my Brother creeping into the bed beside me. He put an affectionate arm around me and snuggled up.

"Pity you fell asleep", he whispered into my ear, "Just after you left, Mary's drawers fell down".

6

Whip behinds

In my young days it was not done for a boy to wear long trousers. Shorts were the thing, just to the knee or just below it, and in the latter instance they were usually fastened with some kind of buckle. These were called knickerbockers. A boy went into long trousers only when he was about to leave school, and then he had his leg pulled unmercifully.

Another rigid convention was the wearing of hats. Everybody without exception wore a hat when out of doors. Children as well as grown-ups. It was just not done to step foot out into the open with the head uncovered. I have even known my Mother put on a hat when popping in to see a neighbour next door. Further, all women wore gloves, even the poorest. To be seen in public without them might class one as a tart; and the word "tart" in those days had the worst possible meaning. The wearing of gloves also had a certain snob value. If a woman wore gloves it was a hint that she did no manual work. Men seldom wore gloves, but they nearly all carried walking sticks. It was the "in" thing to flaunt a walking stick when "dressed for out". There were all kinds of them, and some men owned two or three. A best for Sunday, high-days and holidays, which would often have a gold or silver knob, a good stout stick for walking, with probably a second best and a couple of spares.

Women, at the time I speak of, took enormous care to keep their hats on an even keel. The tiniest slant was discouraged, otherwise it might be suspected that you had had one over the eight. I remember being taken to a concert – they called them "smokers" then – one Saturday night, and one of the comics did a funny monologue about a train smash. One lady, according to his script, called the doctor over just before she died, and said with her last gasp, "Oh doctor! Is my hat on straight?"

They kept their large hats in place with enormous hatpins.

Straw boaters were the trendy things for men. No man was without one. From spring onwards they more or less lived in the things, irrespective of the vagaries of the English summer. Some men of a clerical type attached a cord to the back of their boaters. The other end they clipped on the lapel of their jackets, and this was a safeguard against a windy day. It was not unusual to see a man chasing his straw hat along the street, the hat twirling in the wind, the man puffing hopelessly after it until, perhaps, some well-intentioned person would halt it with his foot. Or it might just be unlucky and finish up under the wheel of a bus.

Some small boys wore boaters too, but the trend was more towards caps.

My Brother sported a mortar-board. These were popular in more refined circles, especially for anyone even remotely connected with ecclesiastical duties, such as a choir boy, which Mother was determined he should one day be.

Brother Fred's mortar-board hat went down well at Hounslow, but when we moved to Chiswick it was a dismal flop. My Brother came home from school the first day crying his eyes out. The boys had enjoyed a red letter day, yanking it off his head by the tassel and playing football with it in the playground.

Mother was incensed.

She went straight round to his school to see the head-master, and after Mother had finished with him he was only too willing to go straight into Brother's classroom and give them a lecture on bad manners the length of which they didn't forget in a hurry. But it made no difference. Brother Fred never wore his mortar-board hat again.

We found Chiswick rather over-powering after the quiet of Hounslow. Mother complained that she didn't know any of the shopkeepers, and was at a loss to find a good butcher. Father told her about the Meat Market, which was reputed to be very good and prices reasonable. He went to a lot of trouble explaining the exact locality, and drew the route for her with his fork on the table cloth.

"You can't miss it, ducks", he said, "You go down some stone steps and the meat is displayed underground, away from the flies and dust".

Mother set off with the plan firmly in mind, and was coyly pleased with herself when she came to a big opening in the middle of the road with steps leading down, just as Father had said. She got about half-way down when a man passing her gave a start, and furnished her with a lecherous grin. She tossed her head and passed him by. At the bottom of the long flight of steps another man, a much nicer type, barred her way and said very gently, "Pardon Madam, I think you've made a mistake. This is a gentleman's place".

"Oh", said Mother, trying to keep control of her equilibrium, "I'm so sorry. I thought it was the meat market".

By that time, she said, her sense of smell told her the plain unvarnished truth, and she went up quicker than she went down.

She was a past-master at getting herself into embarrassing situations. Some years later, during the days of the first world war, she was trying to grope her way into David Greig's grocery store, in the unaccustomed blackout, but stuck right in front of the main entrance was an obstacle which she took to be a peramublator. She put her two hands on it and gave it a push, only to discover it was a man bending down to tie his shoe-lace, and she, in her innocence, was gently pushing him up the behind. He straightened up with an ugly oath, and Mother said, in her most ladylike manner, "So sorry. In the darkness, I mistook you for a pram, and I was feeling for the handle".

Our school at Chiswick was a large County Council affair. It had been built only recently. The going was tough, but there were no two ways about its efficiency. You learnt the three Rs or else. Outside in the playground you were taught the rudiments of rugger, and the school boasted a first class association football side, as it was called, with a first and a second team; both of whom put up a splendid show against another London school soccer side every Saturday morning on different pitches. They played in shirts of yellow and black (half and half), with trousers to the knee, slightly below in fact. I watched them every Saturday without fail, whatever the weather.

Another nice thing about the school, and this I think was universal all over the country, was the wonderful patriotic attitude on Empire Day. We all foregathered in the playground, and we sang "Land of Hope and Glory", at the top of our voices. Everybody had to take a Union Jack flag to school and in both the playgrounds (boys one side, girls the other) it looked just one mass of red, white and blue.

The Union Jack flag was hoisted on the school roof and we all saluted it. It gave us a wonderful thrill, a feeling of belonging.

All schools had their School Inspector. He wore a blue uniform and a hat with a peak, very much like the policeman of to-day. If a child failed to attend school it was the duty of the parents to send a note explaining why. If no note came the Inspector called at the child's house without further delay. He was always an aggressive sergeant major type, and stood no nonsense from parent or pupil. If you were on the sick list he wanted to know quite simply when you would be well enough to return to studies, and had a doctor been called in? He scared the daylights out of the lot of us. Any boy playing truant was a hero indeed. Yet, with all this intimidation, we loved our school. They implanted something within us that, intangible though it was, brought out the true English spirit of Never Say Die. Perhaps it's the old adage of "You've got to be cruel to be kind". I'm not qualified to say, but I do sincerely believe they turned out a generation of people to be proud of.

Outside school hours, my Brother and I learnt a lot of things of a different educational value which we didn't know existed before. For instance, we were initiated into the mysteries and intricate workings of how to acquire what was known in certain coteries of society as a "whip behind". This, in case your knowledge of such things has been neglected, was the art of boarding a vehicle at the rear end without the driver's knowledge and without the formality of paying a fare. If you were lucky you might find a bit of something jutting out of the rear of the vehicle on which you could sit and enjoy your whip behind in comfort. But the chances were that you would have to dig your toes in and hang on for grim death.

It was an exhilerating game, fraught with danger, the worst of which was if some unprincipled lout yelled out from the pavement to the driver of the vehicle, "Whip behind, guv'nor!" Whereupon the driver, who had most likely played the game himself when a boy and knew the ropes, would flick his long whip round the vehicle several times in quick succession, and if you were wise you would depart without further argument. If not, you might get the end of his whip tickling up some part of your anatomy, and the medicine would be repeated until you had given in. This, again, entailed some skill as well as a certain amount of luck, because you had little or no time for your preparation. You could quite easily finish up sprawled flat on your face in the middle of the road embedded in horse dung, and there was always the possibility of an oncoming vehicle running over you into the bargain.

The first "whip behind" I ever had turned out to be a bit of a fiasco. I climbed on the back of a corporation water cart. These carts were literally water tanks on wheels, drawn by a horse. A metal pipe was attached to the rear, which was perforated, and when the driver pulled a handle the water spurted out. It was a very necessary innovation for laying the dust, of which, in summer months, there was plenty.

I had never seen one of these water carts before, and in my innocence I chose this one as my initiation into the glamorous world of whip behinds, despite the frenzied warnings of my older brother and a few of his pals. There was no need for any rotter to shout out "whip behind". The driver of a water cart sat high up and had a perfect view of all that went on around him. I imagine this one could hardly believe his eyes when he saw a little'n of six years be so foolhardy as to squat on the water pipe at the back of his old water cart, and he lost no time in turning on the water.

I was drenched to the skin, and hung about in the street for about two hours afterwards, waiting to dry off before I dared to go home.

Another universally popular game of the day was "marbles". This game was played almost exclusively in the gutter, from a kneeling position. The marble was flicked along by the thumb with the intention of hitting the other boy's marble. If you did so, his marble was yours. Many a boy would travel a quarter of a mile or more playing this game. The only danger was that your marble might go down a drain. If it did, you felt you had been cheated.

I thought up a game that I considered my own copyright. I pinched the basics from some of the gambling machines I had seen set in glass tombs along the seafront at Southend. I carved holes in a cardboard box and invited others to throw a marble through the hole from a distance of about six feet. They were given two marbles if they were successful in getting it through a fairly large hold in the middle, and four if they got one through a smaller hole. I had about four holes altogether with the number of marbles to be won boldly stated above. It became very popular, and soon after I had set up business I had accumulated so many marbles I didn't know what to do with them, for as always it's the bookie who wins in the end. So, I started up a little sideline of my own and sold my newly acquired marbles, cutting the price to about half what they cost in a shop. It was my first taste of big business, and successful beyond my wildest dreams. Mother got a bit worried, however, when boys started knocking on the front door, saying, "Can I have a ha'puth of marbles please?" So my Marble Empire was prematurely nipped in the bud.

Top Spinning was also indulged in by both boys and girls. I never had much patience with it myself, although a thing called a humming top was more exciting because if you could get it really going, it made a lot of noise. There was also a game that came over from France about that time, called Diabolo. A thing like a large cotton reel was tossed in the air by a string held with two sticks, and you endeavoured to catch it as it descended. Its popularity didn't last very long, although, for a while, even grown-ups tried their luck.

Children all played in the streets and it was perfectly safe in every way. There was very little motor car traffic and it was quite a simple matter for a person of any age to cross the road in safety. In fact, a motor car was such a novelty that people would stop in their tracks and watch till it was out of sight. My Mother was genuinely frightened of them. She said, as far as she was concerned, they were wild animals; and she didn't believe that drivers had any control over them whatsoever. If she saw one coming up the main road she would dash into a doorway till it had passed.

It was about this time that I got hopelessly carried away with the magic of Association Football. I begged my Mother to buy me a real football, but this was out of the question owing to price. What she did do however, was to make me a football out of one of Father's old socks. And a very good job she made of it, too. The sock was stuffed tightly with rags, and I used to play with it in the road, in front of our house, and my Brother and a few pals joined in from time to time.

Father used to mend our boots on a last, a three-pronged utensil, each prong shaped to fit a different sized foot. We also wore blakeys in our footwear, small metal pieces with spikes attached for the purpose of hammering them into the sole. They were bought by the card. Each card contained about a dozen different sizes, and cost a penny. Further, and this was pretty general with boys, we wore large round rubber heels on our boots which could be turned round and round as the heel wore down. All rather cumbersome, but they added a long life to the boot or shoe. With the poverty that abounded in those days, this was a big consideration.

Father was now getting nicely on his feet. He was a good salesman, and the job he had brought off demanded a man of personality and one with a gift of the gab.

Which he had in abundance.

One day he decided to go all modern. He shaved off his moustache.

Mother was horrified, and wouldn't let him kiss her. She said he felt naked. We had never seen him without a moustache before. Only very young men were clean-shaven. But this was a new fashion which was beginning to spread. It wasn't many years before hair on the face had become "old hat".

At the time, however, it caused a bit of a sensation. My Brother and I quickly made capital out of it, we told our school chums that our Father was, in reality, a private detective, and that he had shaved off his moustache to disguise himself because he was stalking a dangerous criminal. This gave us tremendous prestige, and surrounded us with an air of mystery.

It was unfortunate that immediately after, Father got the sack.

Once again, he found himself out of a job and being out of work in those days was no laughing matter. There was no National Insurance and no Unemployment Pay. If you were so poor that you were absolutely broke, you had to go on the Panel. It was known as Parish Relief, and you were put through a very severe means test. The alternative was, of course, the Workhouse.

It was at Chiswick that I, for the first time, saw an ambulance. It was a two-wheeled truck with a hood covering the occupant, and was pulled along by two helmeted policemen. It was always followed by a small trail of children, looking apprehensive and forlorn. You would say quietly to whoever happened to be within earshot, "What's happened?" and more often than not the reply would be, "Man cut his throat".

Men seemed always to be cutting their throats. I suppose that when things got hopeless, the old cut-throat razor was an irresistible invitation.

Yet the average man was all against "sticking on the stamps", as it was called when the National Insurance Scheme was at first put forward. I so well remember a couple of years later being taken to see "Dick Whittington", at the Broadway Theatre, Deptford. When it came to the usual community singing, the comedian said, "Now, all those who believe in sticking the stamps on, please sing the chorus". My Mother, my Brother and I sang out at the top of our voices, in accordance with what we knew would be Father's wishes, for he was all for it. But we were on our own. The rest of the audience sat mute until the comedian said, "Those who do *not* believe in sticking on the stamps, please sing this chorus". And the whole audience rose as one man and nearly lifted the roof.

I remember that pantomime so well because I fell for the Principal Boy's big bust. Incidentally, I didn't know it *was* a female, I thought it really was a boy. I was just eight at the time, and it was, I suppose, the first time I had taken stock of such vagaries. For some weeks after, I would be encouraged to talk about it. Any friend of my Mother's calling at the house would be advised, "Get him to tell you about the pantomime".

"Oh?" the caller would say, "What was it like, then?"

"Top-hole!", I would reply with enthusiasm.

"Ask him to tell you about the Principal Boy", Mother would continue, no doubt winking her eye behind my back.

"Oh?" the caller would say again, eyebrows shooting up a bit, "What was the Principal Boy like then?".

"Dick Whittington?" I would query, as though it was the

first time I had considered the matter, "Wonderful! Had a lovely figure too. Right out here".

In course of time I got suspicious of this unwarranted interest in my opinions, and I refused to discuss the matter any further. When the question of pantomime arose, I took no part in the conversation whatever, and I flatly refused to discuss Principal Boys *or* Principal Girls, large bosoms or small bosoms.

As far as I was concerned, the chapter was firmly closed.

Mother always used to say, "When one door closes, another opens", and sure enough, no sooner had Father finished on his salesman job, than a letter came for Mother from a solicitor. It was to say that an aunt of her's had died and left her a legacy of one hundred pounds.

A hundred pounds, in those days, was a lot of money, and Mother and Father put their heads together as to the best way of investing it. Father spotted an advert in the local paper asking for a good salesman to invest a hundred pounds in a Credit Drapery business. He read it out to Mother and they both got rather excited. It stated that the investor, if considered suitable, would be made a third partner in the firm. A weekly salary was to be arranged and, of course, a share in the profits.

"It's what I've wanted all my life", said Father.

A meeting was arranged, Father was engaged, and Mother parted with her hundred pounds. The Credit Drapery business was run by a woman, from her own private residence. She had a male partner whom she called her manager and salesmen were employed to go round to private houses with samples of their goods and take orders for cash. My Father was to be in charge of the salesmen, arranging the various routes and so on.

With Christmas close upon us, my parents invited the Wests to spend it at our house. I have a particularly vivid recollection of that Christmas. It was lovely having Mabel West to play with us, and Frankie was wonderful company. But somehow, although there was much gaiety and laughter, and my Brother and I had more Christmas presents than ever before, I was enveloped in a curious depression which I couldn't shake off.

In the first place, I was disappointed in Christmas Day itself. I could remember previous ones quite well but, for some reason, I got the idea into my head that the day would look different to any other, that it would somehow have a rose-coloured hue. I was just seven, and I presume I had read, for the first time with understanding, all that Christmas entails from a religious point of view. Having worked myself up to what I imagined the day would be like, I was bitterly disappointed when I found out it was just like any other. In the afternoon a nice cold drizzle settled in and we had the lights on in the house from about two o'clock. Added to that, we had rabbit for dinner because we couldn't afford poultry, and after I had carefully placed my two kidneys on the side of my plate to be eaten last (most little boys in those days saved the titbits for last) Frankie West, thinking I didn't like them, ate them himself while I had my back turned talking to Mabel. I finished up the evening crying.

"*Now* what's the matter with him?" demanded Mother, who no doubt had had a trying day.

"It's this Christmas", I howled, "that's what's the matter".

"Christmas?" everyone challenged.

"Yes, Christmas", I asserted, "Why, it's worse than a Sunday".

I must have been incredibly innocent for a child of seven years, for I still thought that boys and girls were made alike. It was Mabel West who unwittingly gave rise to a dark suspicion that all was not as I had believed.

The Wests stayed with us three days, and on their last evening Brother Fred was out at a pal's house enjoying a Christmas party. My Father and Frankie West took themselves off for a drink and Mrs. West, anxious to have a nice little heart-to-heart chat with my Mother during their absence, sent Mabel off to bed early. I was allowed to go to her bedroom to keep her company and have my supper, which happened to be my favourite dish, a piece of Madeira cake. I absolutely adored Madeira cake. I always told my

Mother that when I grew up I should never get married, I would remain loyal to her, no other woman should enter my life. I also used to add, as I munched my Madeira cake with ecstacy, that I would be extremely kind to my children, and bring them all up on Madeira cake.

So, here I was, in Mabel's room, sitting comfortably in front of a nice fire (a special treat as it was Christmas time) munching happily into my Madeira cake.

Mabel was in a particularly jocular mood. It was much too early for sleep, although she had been made to undress and was now in her long flanelette nightgown. She began dancing on the bed, using it as a stage, and characterised all the people she had seen in summer concert parties at Southend-on-Sea. Quite suddenly she lifted her nightgown a little higher than she intended, and I saw something that amazed and puzzled me.

I told my Mother about it the next day.

"Poor girl", I said, "She must have had it cut off and tucked in".

"You were a rude boy to look", my Mother said softly.

It was soon after Christmas that Father began to get suspicious about his new job. "I can't understand it", I heard him say to Mother one night. "People keep calling at the house and abusing me because they've paid for goods and not received them".

"I hope to goodness there's nothing shady", said Mother in alarm.

But there was.

Father turned up one morning, to find all the salesmen gathered outside the house. It was bolted and barred, and there was no sign of the woman or her manager. Some of the salesmen confided in my Father that they had not received their wages for the past two weeks. They seemed to think my Father was responsible, and he had a difficult time explaining that he was, like themselves engaged on a salary. Worse, in fact, because he was the only one to have put money into the firm.

We were having supper one night, Mother was busy frying

some sprats, when a policeman knocked at the front door. Father went and we heard the policeman say something about "them both having been arrested", and that Father was to go to the station with him, as unless he could substantiate his innocence, a warrant for his arrest was also being made out. Father invited him indoors without delay.

He was a big burly policeman, but he had a kind face, and when he smelt the sprats he took his helmet off.

"Would you like a bit of supper?" Mother asked him.

"Smells good", he said, sitting himself down. He made a clean plate of a huge helping that Mother gave him, and while he was eating, Father told him the whole wretched story.

"It's the woman that's the wrong'n" the policeman vouched, smacking his lips, "We've had her inside before. We know nothing of the man, though".

"If you ask me", said Mother, "It's six of one and half-a-dozen of the other".

But father used a more colourful idiom. He said, "in his considered opinion, they were both pissing in the same pot".

Father's intuition proved correct. In fact, they were doing more than that, for it turned out they were a married couple. They got three years a piece in jail for fraud. But poor Mother lost her hundred pounds.

We went through a lean period, but my Uncle Fred came to the rescue. He wrote from Bromley to say he'd fixed my Father up with a job as a milk roundsman, and he could start the very next week.

Mother was distressed.

"You can't walk round Bromley with a milk can in your hand", she said.

"I don't care if I walk round with a jerry in my hand", replied Father, "I want a job".

So, at the weekend, we all went with him to the new Tuppeny Tube station at Turnham Green and waved goodbye.

My Uncle Fred was a master carpenter. He had married a Miss Marshall (my Aunt Emily), whose family ran a well-known laundry at Bromley Common. He wrote to say he had found a house in Bromley that we could rent, and as we had no money to pay for the removal, he would come over to Chiswick with one of the laundry vans and move us himself. Father, of course, was working on his milk round seven days a week and couldn't get away.

Mother was worried because for the first time in her life she had run up an account with the grocer. His shop was at the corner of our road. She had no money to pay him, but to her everlasting credit, immediately she had saved sufficient, she sent it to him by post.

She told all the neighbours Father had pulled off a very good job in Bromley, and how happy she was at going back there, her birthplace, where she had so many wealthy relations and friends. She was a dab hand at carrying things off with a grand manner, and it was a pity that the van which arrived to move us had MARSHALL'S HAND LAUNDRY written in large letters right across both sides of it.

My Uncle brought one of the laundry hands to assist him with the loading up. My Brother and I did our little bit to help and then my Uncle Fred said to us, "Come on, hop up". "I thought we were going by train" we said slightly puzzled.

"No, only me", called out Mother in a loud voice. "We thought you would enjoy the ride in the van more than the train".

We waved goodbye, and as we turned the corner of the road we saw her walking briskly in the opposite direction, towards the station.

We pulled up at the next road, the one that ran parallel to ours, and waited. All of a sudden Mother hove into view.

"Why, there's Mum", we said.

"That's right", said my Uncle, "She's coming in the van with us, but she didn't want the neighbours to know she couldn't afford the train fare".

7

Bromley in Kent

I think some of my happiest boyhood memories are embodied in our lengthy stay at Bromley. Kent was then called The Garden of England and for very good reasons. At the time of which I write, Bromley in Kent was a cosy old country-type town, surrounded by green fields and dewy meadows, alive with colourful butterflies, and dragon-flies with long legs and transparent wings. Wild flowers grew in profusion, and it was a common sight to see children making for home after a long country walk armed with great bunches of all kinds, from buttercups to wild roses. People used to come from miles around, particularly the East End of London, for a day in the country and a good booze up at some of the delightful pubs that abounded. We would see them returning in their horse-drawn vehicles, ecstatically happy and armed with large bunches of colourful flowers, singing away as the sun went down on a glorious summer evening. Every summer seemed to be one long ray of sunshine. It may be just a childhood illusion, but I do well remember our first summer in the town when the evenings remained light until eleven o'clock; some nights later they said we were getting the reflection of the aurora borealis. The sun seemed to shine all the time.

There were fascinating little brooks and miniature rivers, on which we used to float paper-made boats. When we tired of this we would take ourselves off to the many thick-wooded orchards to do a bit of scrumping. Chasing butter-flies with nets, fishing with home-made rods, climbing trees and bird-nesting, we never knew the word "boredom"; life was too full, and it went by oh, so quickly!

On Sunday nights it was a ritual for us to take a long walk with my Uncle Fred and Aunt Emily plus her two daughters. We would start off about teatime and walk four or five miles, over stiles and across unmade paths, without sight of a house. We would sometimes stop to bathe our feet in the cool water of one of the many little streams, which would be teaming with fish, and we would listen to the croaking of the frogs and the incessant song of the birds. As the shadows fell, an occasional bat would zigzag by, which would frighten the ladies no end, in case one got entangled up in her long hair, for this did happen occasionally.

On we would go through spinnies and copses, across fields and meadows, till we came to "a house of call", in other words a country tavern. Here, we kids would stay outside drinking lemonade and eating enormous biscuits, the name of which eludes me; but they were semi-sweet and tasted delicious. In the gathering dusk we would watch the moths dancing in the moonbeams, while our parents refreshed themselves inside the pub, having most likely met a few friends who had also taken a walk but by another route. Then the long trek home in the coolness of the night, so healthily tired we never remembered quite how we got to bed.

Bromley, in those days, took its time.

There was no hurry. Even the manner of speech was leisurely.

Bromley had a character entirely its own. And what's more, it intended keeping it. The electric trams (a great innovation at the time) were allowed to come as far as the bottom of Bromley Hill; there they had to turn and go back. No public transport was allowed to impinge on Bromley soil.

Bromley boasted an excellent market. It was held every Thursday, and literally everything was sold from a pin to an elephant. Market Place in Bromley on a Thursday was the centre of civilisation. Everyone went from miles around.

As a market, it was stupendous. There were the regulars; meat stalls, fish stalls, bric-a-brac stalls and what-have-you, but every week we would have new vendors, "I'm not here to-day and gone tomorrow", types. But for all that, we didn't perhaps see them again. They were travelling salesmen, and only returned if the business warranted it. One of the "regulars" that remains foremost in my memory was a large stall that sold extremely high-smelling hard-boiled sweets (home-made they claimed). One's breath smelt so powerfully after a few of these sweets that a grown-up was apt to remark, "Have you been wasting your money in the market again?" It was an odoriferous advertisement for the stall, albeit a little unpleasant to some.

One of the high spots was the auction of meat late at night. When it was approaching midnight, the head butcher would announce, in his most ear-splitting voice, that the last of the tasty bits were to be sold cheap to avoid storage — there was no deep freeze of course, and women who could really not afford the usual price of meat would wait for this moment and crowd forward to bid.

"Buy, buy, buy, buy!"

You could be lucky and get a real bargain, or you might bid for what looked like a nice joint and go home with a bit of cagmag.

But, come what may, the Bromley Market was the pinnacle of a dog's delight. It was no uncommon sight to see an old stray mongrel (or a young one for that matter) cantering up the street with a nice juicy joint in his mouth. He might be chased by an assistant, but in most cases he outwitted him, and the assistant would return to his stall at a slower pace and with a crest-fallen expression.

Christmas time was the choicest, for then the dogs would have a heyday. A nice fat turkey grabbed by the neck and dragged to some quiet spot was "all the rage". Sometimes another dog, one who was too lazy to go and get his own, would attack the owner for his gains, and most likely while they were fighting it out, some other rotter would sneak up and pinch it. But it was all good fun, an integral part of the catch-as-catch-can convention of Bromley Market.

We stayed in Bromley longer than any place during my youth. Being my Mother's birthplace, she had a very large circle of relatives and friends, all living close at hand. But we didn't settle down right away. The first house we rented displeased Mother because she caught a flea. So we moved to another close by. But Mother said it smelt of cat's widdle, and try as she might, she couldn't get rid of it, so we moved again. "Third time lucky, you see!" Mother said; and Father, who was never so happy as when we were on the go, said, "I don't imagine this will be our last move by a long chalk".

But we all liked the house, and actually we did stay in it for some years. It was a solid old Victorian building, and it nestled in a quiet road just off Bromley Common. There was a large back garden with a huge shed at the rear of it. On opening the back gate one was confronted with an expanse of luscious green meadow which stretched as far as the eye could see. This open space was known locally as Meathrel's field. Mr. Meathrel was our butcher, his shop was just opposite, and Mother observed how strange it was that so many people had names connected with their business.

"Meathrel!" she pondered, "See? Meat!"

Mr. Meathrel had originally bought the fields for the sole purpose of sustaining his horses, of which he had quiet a few. But we boys put them to better and more exciting use in due course.

It was a large three-bedroomed house, with three rooms downstairs and a moderately sized scullery. Houses of any quality boasted a middle room downstairs, and it is hard to know why, for it was hardly ever used. Most people, like us, spent their time in the kitchen, the front room being used only on Sundays or special occasions. The focal point of the whole house was really the kitchen range. In the winter we all sat round it. It threw out an enormous heat and more or less warmed the whole house. Made of cast iron, Mother cleaned it regularly, and thoroughly, with a tin of blacking and a small brush, till you could see your face in it. The oven was large and set in two parts. Everything worthwhile was cooked in it, for Mother had no faith in the new-fangled gas stove.

"Doesn't taste the same", she declared, and Aunt Emily and the others heartily agreed.

By the side of the fire hung the toasting fork. It had five prongs on which you festooned your slice of bread, and you could remove part of the upper range with a "lifter" and toast from there, the danger being that the bread might fall into the fire. Or you could do your toasting in front of the flame, in which case, unless you were pretty expert, you would get a photostat of the protecting bars of the fire across your toasted bread. In either event, you would most likely scorch your hands with the heat. But there was no gainsaying the quality of the toast, when done that way, and the little risks attendant made it all the more enjoyable.

The fire in the range was also ideally suited for the heating of hair curling tongs. All women used them, particularly when "going out dressed".

My Mother had natural roses on her cheeks, but those who's complexions were pale would often wet a bit of red ribbon with their tongue and dab their cheeks with it, for rosy cheeks were fashionable. So were small cupid-bow mouths, but no female used lipstick unless she was one of the "unfortunates of easy virtue".

In front of the kitchen range was a huge fender, on which we could rest our toes. It was large and cumbersome, and needed continuous polishing. All kettles and such were boiled on the range, it was thought extravagant to use gas for such a purpose, and one of the happiest memories I retained was when Mother took a whim for making homemade candy. It was always very sticky and very sweet; but the joy of making it was just wondrous. Next in order of popularity was the baking of potatoes in their jackets. These were done in the oven, well smothered in salt and pepper, and were a special winter-night treat. Occasionally, and always on a Saturday, Mother would buy some muffins from the man who came round the street with a great tray balanced on his head, sounding his bell and shouting, "Muffins and crumpets!" This was sheer ecstacy, especially when one came rushing in from an exciting football match, numbed with the cold and starving hungry.

Practically all one side of the kitchen was taken up with the built-in dresser. Crockery, other than Sunday-best, was displayed there, the cups hanging from little hooks provided for the purpose. As soon as Mother could afford it, she bought herself a treadle sewing machine, which replaced the old table model. It had a small drawer placed at one side, and for some reason this was allotted to me. I was of a thrifty nature, and so Mother gave me an old purse she had finished with to keep my savings in. This I kept in the machine drawer.

My Brother and I were on a weekly basis of one penny each, ha'penny from Father, ha'penny from Mother, which was considered ample pocket money in those days, and with a bit of luck I would pick up the odd ha'penny from a neighbour for running an errand. We were expected to do certain chores to earn our pocket money and these consisted of chopping firewood, cleaning the knives (on a knife board sprinkled with a special powder) tidying up the shed, running errands and any other duty considered prudent. If we defaulted, the money was held back till we came to our senses.

I don't know how I managed to save money, but I did. My purse in the machine drawer always contained a few well-earned coppers. Trouble was, the purse, with its highly-prized contents, was in such a vulnerable position. A tradesman might come to the door unexpectedly and Mother would find she hadn't any small change. So she would borrow what was needed from my purse, sometimes completely forgetting all about it. There would be a dreadful scene later in the week when I might check my cash balance to find it tuppence or threepence short.

So I set up in business as a Money Lender.

My accounts I kept in a small book, small enough in fact to be kept inside the purse. Anyone wishing for a loan took what he wanted, leaving the amount borrowed and his name in the book provided. The borrower was charged one ha'penny interest, irrespective. But it had to be repaid by the weekend.

My Brother was my best customer. Mother, of course, I regarded as a consistent client, and even Father on the odd occasion took advantage of the project. He told all his male friends about it too, and referred to me as "A money lender without balls". This never failed to get a guffaw, and I could never think why.

Shortly after, Brother Fred also set up in business on his own. He purchased a small camera from a toy shop. It cost him sixpence, which he borrowed officially from me. He would spend hours developing the tiny plates in the darkness of the coal shed. These were then placed in a small wooden frame, and the photograph was printed by being placed in a window and exposed to the light for about half-an-hour.

Nothing at all came out at first, then one day . . .

"Eureka!" he cried, "Mother, come quick! I've taken a wonderful photograph of *you*".

He danced about like a cat on hot bricks, and we all gathered at speed.

"Is that me?" queried Mother when she saw it.

"Yes. Isn't it great? Even the shine on your shoes, the spots on your dress. Everything! Unfortunately, I didn't get your head in".

His photographic technique improved and he decided to turn his gift to monetary use. One of his contemporaries, whose name was Abba (at least, that's what we called him), had a great ambition to be a professional footballer when he grew up. His favourite position was that of the goalkeeper, and he approached my Brother regarding the possibility of

70

his being photographed leaning against the goalpost.

"No problem at all", vouchsafed Brother Fred. "We have a long thin stump of tree in our back garden which will photograph for all the world like a goalpost. What time shall I expect you?"

Abba duly turned up, all spick and span in a nice white jersey, which is what goalkeepers habitually wore then, and after Mother had been persuaded to remove her washing from the tree trunk, which was what it was normally used for, Abba folded his arms and posed for the camera with a fetching smile.

He was on the doorstep first thing next morning all agog to see how he looked when facing the world as a professional goalkeeper. It was more than a bit blurred, and there was no mistaking the slightly bent tree trunk for what it was. But my Brother was optimistic.

"Excellent, don't you think?" he said brightly.

Abba's face fell, and he hummed and hawed. "You wouldn't know it was me", he said half heartedly, "would you?"

My Brother looked at it over Abba's shoulder and cocked his head at an angle, "Oh yes", he said, "I can see it's you all right. Just like you, in fact".

"How much is it?" murmured Abba dejectedly.

"Oh, I don't know," replied my Brother, as though he'd been too busy to even think about it before. "Give me sixpence, that'll do".

Abba parted with his sixpence and faded slowly away; rather like a man in a dream.

Meantime, Father was settling down well in his role as a milk roundsman. His call of duty took him to many of the best families living in Bickley and Chislehurst, the elite part of the district, and although his business brought him into contact with the "downstairs" fraternity only, he found them possessed of considerable charm and wit. He liked them, and they adored him; for he was a man of great character and a tremendous sense of humour. So much so, that when later he was offered the post of Manager/Foreman, which meant he would be confined to office and shop duties, he refused.

Milk carts in those days were shaped something like a Roman chariot, and drawn by a horse. The milkman carried a great can of milk to the door of the customer, and with a skimmer he ladled out the milk into a jug which the customer provided. Much banter would ensue during the operation, and this suited my Father to a T. When rain fell it was the custom to say, "This'll make the milkmen open their cans!" For it was firmly believed, and probably not without reason, that milkmen watered their milk; thereby making a nice little bit on the side. Whether that was so, I am not qualified to say. But Father certainly seemed to be quite affluent for a man earning 25/- a week.

It wasn't long before he bought us a brand new piano. A lovely rosewood upright, and it cost £18. I still have the receipt to prove it; and what's more, I still have the piano. It is now a handsome period piece, and still retains a good tone.

He bought something else too, around about that time. Something which brought us great solace and love for many years to come. He stalked in one day fresh from the dairy and flung a small puppy on the meal table. We had just sat down to tea, and Mother's protestations were eclipsed by our hoots of delight.

"They were going to drown the little beggar", said Father, "so I gave the lad a penny for it".

Regretfully, in those days, puppies and kittens, in fact even quite big dogs and cats, were habitually drowned when not wanted. There were no vets as we understand them to-day, and in any case people were, for the most part, too poor to spend money in such a way. So there was no alternative.

We hugged Father, and we hugged the dog. We immediately named it "Feller", despite the fact that it was palpably a female. Mother, in fact, was wont to call it "Boy" when it matured; she said the one syllable carried better when she was hailing it from a distance. I often wonder in retrospect what passers-by must have thought as Mother would shout at the top of her voice, "Boy, boy, boy! Come here!" It must have been particularly bewildering when Feller was in the family way, which was quite often, with her udders hanging low.

She grew into a pretty little dog, despite the fact she was a mongrel many times over, and she caused quite a sensation once on polling day. My Father, being an ardent Liberal supporter, had infused us all with his radical enthusiasm. In our front room window we had hung a large oval shaped Show Card advocating Mr. Lely, the Liberal candidate, as the right man to represent us in Parliament. On polling day we cut out the photograph of Mr. Lely, which was in the centre of the Show Card, and Feller's head was pushed through the hole in its place. We paraded her on a lead through the main streets of Bromley, supported by a few of our pals. It no doubt looked a little odd, Feller's head protruding through the Card amongst all the Liberal propaganda, proclaiming in large block letters:— THIS IS THE MAN.

But we meant it well.

And we sung our Liberal War Cry as we marched her at the head of the procession:—

"Vote, vote, vote for Mister Lely,
Kick old Forster out the door,
For Lely is the man,
And we'll have him if we can,
And we won't vote for Forster any more."

Despite our valient efforts, it was Mr. Forster, the Conservative candidate, who got in.

8

Entertainments *Alfresco*

Organised entertainment when I was a kid was not very popular. In fact, it was hardly ever attempted. We made our own fun. Girls of all ages, and all classes, were adherents to the skipping rope, either singly or in bulk. They skipped mostly in the streets, where all children played, and with every degree of safety.

Hoop bowling was popular. Girls walloped wooden hoops along with a slender wooden "beater". Boy's hoops were made of iron and they coaxed them along with a thing we called a skid. We would often run miles spinning our hoops. In the autumn the game of conkers was in favour. All kinds of methods were employed to add substance and strength to a conker from heating it in the oven to soaking it in mysterious oils. To play the game, you made a hole through the middle and inserted a piece of string. Each lad took a turn having a bash at the other's, and according to how many your conker smashed, so its value grew. It became a one-er, a two-er or a three-er, etc. If you smashed one which claimed to be, say, a sixer and yours was already a four-er, then your's became a ten-er. You were "on your honour" to tell the truth regarding your conker's history. No boy on his honour would tell a lie. Sometimes, if the occasion was very great, a boy would have to swear "over his Mother's grave" (despite the fact that she might still be alive).

"Comic Cuts", and "Chuckles" were the only two comics of the day. Later on, a boy would read "The Magnet", and if he wanted adventure stories he might take "The Boy's Own". These, as far as memory serves me, were the only publications for boys.

"The Boy's Own" would sometimes publish a short play, and it was this that gave us the idea of turning our shed, at the bottom of the garden, into a miniature theatre. One half of the shed housed the audience and the other half was the stage. Two discarded window curtains were strung on to a piece of wire for use as the Front Curtain, and a couple of sacks were sewn together to partition off a tiny dressing room. The audience paid a nail, a fagcard or, perhaps, a piece of string; in fact anything useful gave the right of admittance. They sat on beer crates, or empty boxes, and when these were fully occupied, they sat on the dusty floor.

No one ever complained.

The plays themselves were always exciting. Sometimes heroic, sometimes romantic. The players weren't always sure of their lines, and so the "book" was placed on the floor between the actors and the audience. Rather like the modern "idiot board" used in current television programmes, except that in our case the actor might resort to a kneeling position owing to the smallness of the print.

It was winter time when this thespian project first came into being, and bitterly cold. But the size of the audiences was such that overheating was the only danger, not to mention a slight irk from body odours. Indeed, the pressure was so great that at times the audience spilled over on to the stage.

Our main difficulty was the lack of actors. Many wished to watch, but few were sufficiently enthusiastic when it came to the arduous business of rehearsals. Apart from that, in most cases they were incredibly self-conscious and few indeed had any talent whatsoever.

It was, therefore, with polite caution that we greeted a small boy who one day came forward and offered us his services. He was well-known to us all. His name was Sidney Jones, but he was cited universally as "Kiggy Yones", for the very simple reason that he had a pronounced impediment in his speech. He suffered from what was diagnosed in those days as having "no roof to his mouth". When asked his name, he would reply, "Kiggy Yones".

So the cast gazed at Kiggy with a certain amount of askance. Acting with an impediment as pronounced as his was fraught with dark possibilities.

We wandered off into a huddle.

"Would you have any objection to playing 'Lady' parts?" he was asked, after a bit.

He said he wouldn't object.

We huddled again.

"No one ever wants to play Lady parts", my Brother whispered. We nodded our heads apprehensively.

Kiggy was then asked if he would be prepared to take a Lady part home with him and see what he could do with it.

He promised he would. So he was engaged "on appro."

We got busy immediately, making Kiggy a wig. This we designed out of combed rope, and Mother gave us an old frock she had finished with which we cut down to Kiggy's dimensions. However, he was such a very small boy that the frock, even when cut completely in half, on him looked ridiculous (if that is the right word). So Mother was prevailed on again and came up with a rather gaudy pink blouse, which on his frail body came almost to the ground. My Brother said it would never be noticed, and as our audience were not the fussy type, we let him wear the blouse without a skirt. I was commissioned to step out in front of the curtain before the play began to make an announcement.

"Ladies and gentlemen", I said (we had one small girl amongst the audience) "We trust you will excuse the heroine not wearing a skirt, as owing to unforeseen circumstances, he has not been fitted for one".

Up to a point, of course, this was true. Strange to say, the announcement brought forth a round of applause. Our audiences were always unpredictable.

The performance itself must have been hilarious by normal standards. My Brother breathing tender symbols of love down the heroine's neck, and "her" replying in words so distorted that she might have been telling him to go to hell. But our audience never flinched. They sat on the edge of their boxes with ears akimbo, and lapped it up.

Kiggy's disability had one advantage, no one could prove whether he was saying the right lines or not. And we didn't have to be too fastidious about cues. You just waited till Kiggy stopped talking, then you nipped in.

The appetite of our audience was insatiable. We just couldn't get enough plays to satisfy them. So we hit on another idea which, to say the least, was a trifle macabre.

We called it "A Hanging Exhibition".

A gallows was fashioned and erected in the centre of the shed. The audience stood in a circle round it and watched goggle-eyed. Pongo, who, with bits of material added to his person year by year, had now grown in stature sufficiently to sport an old jacket and a cut-down pair of Father's trousers, was brought into service as "the victim".

The early proceedings of the case were rather arbitrary and varied according to the day's whim, but the spectacle of the actual hanging never failed to cause a stir. Many came to watch and ponder again and again.

Pongo, with a rope firmly about his neck, was asked with great solemnity if he had anything to say before just sentence was passed. Another voice, one on behalf of Pongo, would pipe up and say with great thoroughness,

"I am innocent!"

He would then be hanged without delay and his body cut down and placed in a large cardboard box. A funeral procession followed, in which the audience participated, and we all trouped round the garden, finishing up by the side of a large hole which had previously been dug for the purpose. My

Brother, dressed now as a priest, would read the last rites (or what he knew of them) and someone would be cued to dash forward and announce in a dramatic voice that we had got the wrong man. Whereupon, the cardboard box was opened up and artificial respiration employed.

It was a winner all the way.

As winter turned to spring, and spring turned to summer, we searched our brains for something a little different.

"What about a concert party, like they have at Southend?" my Brother said one day.

"In the open air?"

"In our back garden".

"What about a stage?"

We walked around the streets thinking.

Inspiration always comes like manna from heaven if you have faith and are sufficiently in earnest. A few of us were snooping round a large gentleman's house, which was being converted into a Clarke's College, when one of us noticed an enormous window frame lying on the grass. It had obviously been discarded. It measured about nine feet both ways, and was embellished with little angels and things, all standing out in high relief. In one voice we said it.

"An alfresco stage prescenium!"

We numbered a crowd of over half-a-dozen, but it took all our combined strength to carry the thing home. People stared a bit as we passed, and Charlie Pattern said,

"I wonder if they'll put us in the nick for stealing?"

But his brother Norman said, "Who'd want a great thing like this?" And my Brother said, "Don't worry, they'll never miss it".

So, puffing and blowing, we got it to our back garden and then began to discuss ways and means of hoisting it up.

The best way, we decided, was to tie it from its top to the fence at either side of the garden. This worked like a charm. We supplied the nails, and Charlie Pattern supplied the rope.

Charlie was my Brother's age. A cheeky-faced boy with dazzling blue eyes and a ruddy complexion. He bubbled with youthful enthusiasm, had a natural-born charm and, what was more important from our point of view, he was devoid of any kind of conscience.

His mother was a widow. She owned the paper shop across the road, and in addition to selling tobacco and confectionery she also kept a good stock of toys and novelties. When anything a bit untoward was needed, Charlie could always supply it. It was simply a matter of waiting till his mother's back was turned.

The platform was designed from two old doors that we scrounged. These balanced precariously on a jumble of beer crates and biscuit tins. The backcloth consisted of strips of disused sacks, with here and there a selection of Flags of all Nations.

It looked a bit garish, but my Brother said, "In the strong sunlight it will all merge".

Charlie supplied the flags, and he also fitted us up with some paper hats shaped in the mould of an admiral's. These we wore as our uniform. Not entirely in keeping, but it was all Charlie could lay his hands on.

The cast consisted of six boys, all of whom could sing and dance about a bit, and Kiggy Jones was retained as the "Lady". In all professional summer concert parties in those days, the cast was all male with one exception; the lady usually being programmed as "A Serio Comic". And that's what Kiggy was.

The programmes (which were changed continuously) consisted of solos, trios and sketches, with an occasional vocal concerted. We had no instrument to guide us, and it was no uncommon thing for one half of the stage to be singing in a slightly different key from the other half. But our audience did not suffer from a surfeit of musical sensitivity. In fact, if it was a song they knew, they would often join in lustily, and mostly likely in a different key again. But we usually finished up in unison. It was a question really of which lot could belt it out the loudest; sooner or later the others would fall into line.

When enthusiasm for the concerts began to wane we decided to turn our back garden into a boxing booth. The stage platform was dragged to the centre of the garden and augmented, whilst Charlie supplied two pairs of boxing gloves and some more rope.

The public, who peeped in from time to time, waited expectantly, for there was no doubt we had become big business. My Brother began to take on the look of the ever-worried impresario, and his manner became expansive. In the middle of hammering in a few nails he would say to me, "Go up the house and fetch such and such a thing". The house, of course, was only a few feet distant, but it sounded big and grand, as though we lived in a mansion some few acres away, and secretly I enjoyed the whimsy.

The fights were organised according to age and weight, and my Brother (who disliked getting hurt) appointed himself referee. Unfortunately, at the first exhibition, one of my Brother's contemporaries was without a partner, so I was asked if I would step into the breach rather than disappoint him. I wasn't much more than half his size, and I had a clear understanding with him before the fight that it would be purely a "sparring match", just slapping each other's arms a bit and shuffling around to make it look good.

We stepped up briskly each to the other when our match was announced, and shook hands in a gentlemanly manner. I had hardly got into my animal-crouching-position, at which I rather fancied myself when doing this sort of thing, before he lambed out and socked me soundly on the nose. I gazed back at him through running eyes and said, "Steady on!"

And he hit me again.

From then on it was purely a matter of me running round the ring with him chasing after me.

My Brother, watch in hand, stopped the fight a trifle prematurely and, raising both our right hands in the air, declared the match "a draw".

The annual School Sports, in which all the schools in the district took part, inspired us to run our own sports day in Meathrel's Fields. Long jumping, high jumping, three-legged, egg-and-spoon and the sack races were all included in the schedule, as well as the usual sprints of a hundred yards and two-twenty, with a special endurance race of three times round the field for the big boys. The running was made all the more exciting by the fact that someone might slip head-over-heels in a dollop of horse dung partly hidden in the long grass.

Charlie Pattern had a busy time obtaining sufficient prizes to go round, many of which he won back himself. The prizes were presented in our back garden, my Brother and the rest of the "Committee" sitting on what had once been the boxing ring, with the prizes proudly displayed on an old wooden bench in front of them.

The venture was such a success that we repeated the experiment the following week. This time hordes of enthusiasts turned up, some ready clad in their vests and running shorts, and some accompanied by their mums, who had come to look on.

Extra "heats" had to be arranged to cope with the unexpected numbers. Extra prizes for 2nds and 3rds were planned, and Charlie Pattern was noticed to be missing for some considerable time. (If ever his mother indulged in an orgy of stock taking, she must have had a shock).

Even my Mother and Father, who normally watched our vagaries surreptitiously from the privacy of the scullery window, came boldly out through the back garden gate and took a lively interest in the proceedings.

The foray was in full swing when Feller, our little mongrel dog, somehow got loose. She was always at the height of emotion when she saw people running or jumping about. The hundred yards' sprint had just commenced, about twenty boys were racing each other as though their very lives depended on it. Onlookers were jumping up and down, yelling and shouting. Feller sensed something was wrong. In her doggy mind she attributed the trouble to Mr. Meathrel's horses. She chased after them, yapping and snapping at their heels. The horses fled in all directions, rushing hither and thither and getting hopelessly mixed up with the runners.

It was sheer chaos!

But it all stopped very suddenly. Mr. Meathrel and two of

his assistants appeared on the scene, each brandishing a large stick.

We left the field in haste, not to say ignominy. The only one to remain was Feller. She stuck to her guns with fervour and valiance, even when one of Mr. Meathrel's assistants threw his boot at her.

Mr. Meathrel approached my Father.

"If I ever catch one of your boys in my field again", he said, trying hard to get his wind back, "I'll have the law on yer, see if I don't".

"Silly old fool", said Father when he'd gone, and then added, rather unfairly I thought, "Trying to tell *me* about the law? He doesn't know 'A' from a bull's foot".

9

Relatives' values

My Mother was easy.

I could, as a rule, twist her round my little finger. Only on two special occasions did I ever go down on my knees to her in earnest supplication. The first time I won (at least I think I won), and the second time I quite definitely lost.

The first plea was on humanitarian grounds, and concerned a small mouse who was squatting in the mousetrap awaiting execution in a bucket of water. On a previous occasion I had witnessed the demise of a little mouse by this barbaric method and the sight had sickened me. I had made up my mind, there and then, to devote my life to the saving of all mice from such watery fates in the future. I took my Mother's two hands in mine and I fell on my knees.

"Please", I pleaded, "Don't drown it".

My Mother hesitated, and I thought I felt a slight sympathetic tightening of the hands.

"They're only vermin", she faltered.

"They have feelings, same as us". I persisted, and out of the corner of my eye I fancied I saw the mouse listening with ears a-twitching. "Let it go".

My Mother looked hard at me, and then said, "All right, you get off to school and I'll set it free".

"Promise?"

"I promise".

"On your word of honour?"

"Yes".

No person in the world in which I lived in those days would go back on their word of honour, so I left for school with a light heart.

"Did you free the mouse?" was my immediate demand on my return home.

"Yes", my Mother responded. "As soon as you had gone, I took the trap to the end of the garden and released the mouse. By now it will have settled down in somebody else's house".

Inwardly and very privately, I offered up a silent prayer of thanks to God.

"You think it will live and be happy?" I asked.

"I'm sure it will", she asseverated. And I believed her implicitly. But in retrospect, I have a sneaky feeling she had the same artful grin on her face that had betrayed my Father on a future occasion.

The second incident was a more mundane affair and had a purely selfish motive as its goal. I say "goal" in all sincerity, for it concerned a football match. Bromley had been drawn to play at home to the London Caledonians in the Amateur Cup. They were old rivals, and I had anticipated the match with suppressed excitement for some time. And as though fate were on my side, I had run into Charlie Pattern the night before the day of the game and he had offered me a ticket giving free entrance to the ground as he had two and didn't know what to do with the other one.

I awoke the next morning after a restless night's sleep, looked out of the window and there it was — raining cats and dogs. Being Saturday, I had my chores to see to. I prayed very fervently to God to stop the rain in time for the match, as I set about my tasks with added ardour. But apparently he was not in a receptive mood, for by lunchtime, it was raining harder than ever, and outside everything was literally swimming about. Torrents of water were lashing against the windowpane, driven there by a maddening half-gale.

I gathered myself as the clock struck two and approached my Mother, complete in my school cap and Sunday overcoat.

"Goodbye Mum", I said, as casually as I could.

She affected not to hear. So I said it again.

"Where do you think you're off to?" she said, a bit testily.

"The football match", I said, trying to look surprised that she didn't know.

"You're not going to any football match in this weather", she retorted hotly. "Are you mad?"

"It's the Cup Tie", I wailed.

"I'll see your neck as long as my arm first", she replied, matching her voice with mine.

It was then I did it.

Down I went, clutching the calves of her legs, tears in my eyes. "You don't understand", I whispered in a theatrical voice.

"Oh yes I do", she countered, in a perfectly natural voice. "I understand that you will stand there in the pouring rain like the silly little fool that you are, pretending to enjoy the football and catching your death of cold into the bargain. No, you are not going!"

I cried, I screamed, and I cajoled. But Mother would not give way. I followed her about the room on my knees.

"Many a death caught on a football field", was all I could get out of her as she went around dusting the ornaments.

So, for once, my histrionics failed to do the trick, and Bromley lost the match, two goals to one.

"Here's a penny", said my Father, "Pop over to the Saddlers shop and get me a tin of Elbow Grease."

Such were the tricks we all got up to on April Fool's Day. Some of them were quite elaborate and took a deal of pre-planning, and it was quite a common sight to see a city gentleman complete with top hat and frocktail coat dashing off to catch his train with a long paper tail pinned on behind him. I remember once trying to pin a piece of cardboard on my choir master's back on which I had written "kick me". But he caught me in the act and having no sense of humour fined me a shilling on the spot.

"Don't be long, I need it in a hurry", continued my Father as I sped out of the front door.

The man in the saddler's shop looked hard at me over his glasses.

"Who's it for?" he said, suspiciously.

"My Father, " I said brightly, "and he wants it in a hurry."

"Well, I'm right out of elbow grease", he mused, "Tell you where you will get it though, try the off licence. Ask to see the manager, Mr. Tossit. Tell him I sent you".

The lady at the off licence was of the formidable type. She fixed me with a beady eye. "What do you want him for?" she asked.

"I want some elbow grease", I said, "And the man at the saddler's shop said Mr. Tossit would fix me up with a tin".

"Well he's having a lie down right now and doesn't want to be disturbed", she said disagreeably, "And his name isn't Tossit, it's Thomset".

"So sorry," I said, and coughed politely into my hand.

She went away, and shortly after Mr. Thomset appeared, looking a bit dishevelled and scratching a mop of untidy hair.

"Well", he said sharply, "What is it?"

"I want a tin of elbow grease please, and it's rather urgent, it's for my father."

Mr. Thomset stopped scratching his head and leaned forward with both hands on the counter.

"Who sent you to me?" he asked in a hoarse whisper.

"The gentleman at the saddler's shop".

"Oh, he did, did he!" And he clucked his tongue and nodded his head up and down several times. "Tell you what, son. Do you know the Penny Bazaar?"

Well, of course, I knew the Penny Bazaar, everybody did. It was a kind of fore-runner of Woolworths, with lots of small counters dotted about displaying the most fascinating things of every description, everyone of which was priced at a penny. It was a small boy's paradise, and a delightful place in which to shelter from the rain.

"You mean the one in the market place?" I enquired.

"Of course it's the one in the market place", he snapped, "There's only one of 'em in Bromley, isn't there?" And then added, "I can see you'll never set the Thames on fire".

"Do you think they'll have a tin there?" I asked anxiously.

"Positive", he smirked. "They sell everything, don't they?"

So off I went with alacrity.

The Market Place was a good mile distant, so I ran most of the way. I approached the girl standing behind the counter, with a lack of breath and a red face. She was a young girl, and spoke with a pronounced Kentish accent.

"I ain't never 'eard of it", she said, looking at me as though I smelt nasty. "What you reckon it's called, then?"

"Elbow grease", I repeated, raising my voice, "It's grease in a tin, and the manager at the off licence said you sold it".

"Well I ain't never 'eard of it", she said again, and with that the supervisor passed by. We both explained our dilemma to her in our own respective ways and at the same point of time. The supervisor then bent down low and placed a fist under my nose.

"This is elbow grease", she said, waving her fist up and down and extending her arm muscles. "Don't you come in here, young man, trying to make April Fools of us. Get out before I call a p'liceman!"

I ran all the way back home, and I burst into tears when I got there.

"You can keep the penny", said Father pleasantly.

And then I laughed with the rest of them.

"It's no good 'em dying on a Wednesday mate. They won't have time to lay 'em out till Sunday!"

So spoke my Uncle Fred when referring to the employees of Marshall's laundry, which was owned by his wife's Mother.

Mrs. Marshall, Senior, had started the laundry many years

before in her own scullery, assisted by the older children of her ever increasing family. She must have been a good washerwoman, for, by the time of which I write, Marshall's Laundry was a byword "up Bromley Common", and did for all the best families in Bickley and Chislehurst also. It was sub-titled a Hand Laundry which meant I suppose that all ironing and delicate work was done by hand and not by machinery as now. The laundry stood in its own grounds and employed about twenty laundresses. The "washing", as it was always called, was dried and aired within the precincts of the grounds, and then hung out on dozens of clothes lines, all braced up by the old-fashioned garden-type of wooden prop. They possessed three large vans and six horses.

It was a very busy laundry, and all Mrs. Marshall's daughters worked in it including my Aunt Emily, who was her eldest. It was pointless calling on my Aunt Emily on Friday nights, she had no time for idle conversation, she was up to her eyes doing the books. She would oftimes be in a suppressed rage and, if you cared to believe the veracity of my Uncle Fred, she was sometimes known to call the cat in from outside for the sole purpose of kicking it out again.

She had a younger sister who was married and lived a few doors away. Her name was Gert. According to legend, Gert had a baby every nine months. She would give birth to the child and within the hour she would be found sitting up in bed folding "smalls". Much of this, of course, is speculative, and needs taking with a grain of salt, but there is no doubt that the whole family worked like Trojans, for to them Marshall's Laundry was the centre of civilisation. The laundry, and the grounds adjoining, backed on to my Aunt Emily's house. She had two daughters named Vera and Nora who were about my age, and I often went with them into the laundry environs to play games. The laundry itself was rather frightening, with huge vats of dirty-looking water and a curious smell of soap suds and sweaty clothes. But it was a wonderful media for the game of hide-and-seek, the only miracle being that none of us ever got drowned, for some of the places we hid in were perilous beyond belief.

My Uncle Fred had no teeth worthy of the name. A few black stumps on which he managed to masticate his food and support his pipe, which was hardly ever out of his mouth.

"You must see a dentist, Fred", my Mother would say every so often, "You really must! Have those awful old black stumps out, and a nice set of white falsies put in".

But Uncle Fred was a coward. He couldn't face the dentist.

"I manage all right mate", he would say, smiling broadly and exposing the awful black mess, "I've got two good teeth in my head and thank God they face each other, so I can chew my victuals without inconvenience."

But one night we popped in for a chat, as we often did, and Uncle Fred was sitting there with a great mouthful of artificial teeth but, alas, no pipe in his mouth.

"I've had 'em all out mate", he said (with difficulty).

Aunt Emily then took up the tale, in between her household chores.

It appears that an itinerant dentist had called one day at the house, removed all his old stumps, and supplied him with a full set of artificial teeth by the simple expedient of trial and error. The whole thing was done on the spot, and cost him one pound. In those days, these parasites of society used to go round from house to house looking for victims. Any gullible person might be persuaded into having unwanted teeth removed, and false ones put in in their place, by these unqualified quacks. They carried a large selection of false teeth in their packs, many of which had, no doubt, been rescued from deceased people.

So, there my Uncle Fred sat, with his two sets of artificial teeth (top and bottom), without power of speech, unable to eat, unable even to smoke his pipe.

We had to laugh although we felt sorry for him. It was so typical.

"Persevere" warned Mother, "Don't take them out whatever you do. Sleep in them if necessary".

My Uncle Fred replied with a glassy eye.

We called in on him again a few days later. He greeted us with a large toothless smile.

"Where's your teeth?" asked Mother.

"In the dustbin mate", replied Uncle Fred, "I get on better without 'em". And for the rest of his life that's exactly what he did, living to a ripe old age.

Like many men of his day, he was curiously unworldly for, apart from holidays, people as a rule travelled little. Uncle Fred could never believe that folk who lived in Glasgow, for instance, were much the same in every respect as people who lived in London. He fondly imagined that they sat about on hills of heather singing Scottish songs, all wearing kilts.

My Aunt Emily was even less informed. She thought once you went north of London you found yourself very quickly in a kind of woodland thicket, and if you were lucky enough to come across a human being, he would probably speak pidgin English.

Yet Aunt Emily had an extraordinary sense of humour, and I used the phrase "extraordinary" in every sense of the word. Simple everyday humour that amused other people left her stone cold, but anything singular, especially if a little sad, would probably send her into convulsions. As, for instance, when I used to stand up and sing a song "written and composed by myself".

10

Spiffing Saturdays

We didn't eat a lot of sweets when I was a boy. For one thing it was considered bad for our health, and for another we couldn't afford them. Not that they were expensive judged by modern standards. Most lines suitable for children were sold at a penny per quarter, and chocolate bars were a ha'penny each or a penny for a large one.

One special treat for a child was to have an orange with a piece of lump sugar inserted half-way in it. You sucked the orange juice through the sugar. It was spiffing! But oranges were only obtainable round about the Christmas period, when they were in season; not all the year round as now.

However, apples being home-grown could be had all the time, and were comparatively cheap. For all that, a boy munching an apple in the street would often be followed by another boy beseeching him for the core. If the owner of the apple was a decent chap, he would leave an appreciable amount of juicy substance adhering, but if he was a cad he might eat the lot, leaving just the stringy bits for the other to do the best he could with.

Sometimes my Mother would wrap up a few currants in a piece of paper in lieu of sweets, and off I'd go to school, happy as a sand boy. Occasionally too, she would sprinkle some castor sugar on a piece of bread, for I was a hell of a "sweet tooth". But, on the whole I think children ate better food than they do to-day, even the poorest. There was nothing synthetic, it was good wholesome food and very nourishing. People indulged themselves at the weekend, more especially on Sundays. But as a general rule a joint of meat was a once-a-week affair. In between, one could buy rabbits cheaply, and sausages (really meaty ones) were constantly on the menu. Roly-poly pudding was high up the charts in popularity, only superceded by a dish known as Treacle Pudding, but which was in actual fact suet dumplings smothered in golden syrup. The best way to insult most boys, and me in particular, was to plant a nice dish of creamy rice pudding in front of him. We hated it!

Saturday was the red letter day of the week as far as I was concerned. It was an incredibly busy day. Having got my chores done in the morning, I would hasten to the rec' to see my school team play soccer; home for lunch, then rush off to see the local club play football in the afternoon. Bromley boasted quite a good soccer team and occasionally came up against the professionals when competing for the London Cup. I would race up Hayes Lane, where the pitch was, on my way home, and anyone attending his garden would be told the result of the match (as a rule, much to his surprise; especially if he was an ardent gardener and not interested in football as such).

After tea we would all make for Bromley High Street where the majority of people were doing their week's shopping. The shops were open quite late, some till midnight, and it was all very gay, with tradesmen yelling the quality of their goods and bright lights everywhere. Crowds milling around and friends meeting friends.

On the way home we would break the journey at the pub for a drink. Our favourite call was Blower Browns. I don't suppose he was christened "Blower", but that's the name by which he was known. Children were allowed inside pubs in those days, and when the law put a stop to this, many youngsters could be seen on a Saturday night playing about outside the pubs waiting for their parents to come out. It's doubtful which was the lesser evil.

The strange part is, that very few women went into pubs, even in those days. It was "not done". My Mother hated the idea. She was a strict teetotaller. She broke the pledge purely through unforeseen circumstances.

For some time her health had been a little impaired, or to use the current idiom, she had been a little seedy, not up to scratch. The doctor said that she was anaemic and prescribed Iron Jelloids. But these didn't do any good so she went on a course of Doctor William's Pink Pills for Pale People. Still she was "off song". So her doctor then advised her to drink a glass of Guinness each night, but first she had to heat a poker in the fire and when red hot dip it in the Guinness. This, he reckoned, would put some iron in her blood.

To her everlasting shame she became addicted to the habit. Or, as my Father was wont to say in his jocular manner, she got the flavour for it. It was her one naughty indulgence. Every night, before retiring, she imbibed a glass of Guinness. The anaemia left her, and the red hot poker became a thing of the past, but the bedtime glass of Guinness remained.

And so, on Saturday nights, she would carry the indulgence one step further by quaffing her Guinness in a pub. But the general procedure was not as straightforward as that. Mother was convinced people would be spying on her from behind heavily curtained windows and saying, "My God, there's a woman going into a pub". It would take the combined persuasion of my Father plus my Uncle Fred and a few of his boozing pals to allay Mother's fears. All the way there Mother would reiterate, "Do you think anyone will see me?"

"What if they do?" Father would reply.

"That's not the point", Mother would argue.

"Women do go in pubs now", my Uncle Fred would coax, "That's why they have saloon bars".

"Are you sure?"

"Of course", they would all chorus.

We would get as far as the saloon bar door and Mother would hang back.

"Have a look and see if there is anyone who might recognise me", she would instruct Father. Father would open the door, take a hasty look inside and say "No one". A gangway would then be made for Mother to proceed, ladies always went first, and she would get half in the door and then jump back.

"I can't", she would say, "Not tonight".

It was then the duty of all concerned to persuade her in the loudest terms possible (for the sake of any passers-by) that she was a good woman and doing no harm. Whereupon, she would quietly slither in and hurry to the darkest corner, with her head held low.

When asked what she was "going to have", she would reply in a firm voice that she never drank. It was then incumbent upon Father to woo her into experimenting with a glass of Guinness, which the doctor had prescribed, and which would do her good. When the drink was placed on the table in front of her the ritual would start all over again. All present would be expected to plead with her, until at last she would lift her veil, drape it coyly over her nose, and take a tiny sip. She would then screw up her face as though in mortal agony, and the veil would be quickly dropped again. This charade went on all through my boyhood days, and I used to watch with admiration and secret amusement.

All Saturday night I would pre-arrange my soccer match to be held the following day by my imaginary team which I called the Roman Rovers. Though purely a figment of my imagination, this football team lived in my mind most vividly. I knew all their names and held a precise mental picture of each one's appearance. A detailed record in a special book was kept concerning all their matches. They played in blue jerseys with a white band round the middle, and I was their stunningly clever centre forward. The matches took place in the back garden, up and down the pathway. We drew enormous crowds, for we hardly ever lost. On one occasion my enthusiasm prompted me to draw a picture of the spectators on the garden fence in chalk. Hundreds and hundreds of little heads. It took me hours. When Father saw it I washed it out in a matter of seconds, with a scrubbing brush and a bucket of hot water.

As a team we must have been ahead of our time, for not only did we play in the first division but we also took part in a "World League", in which we came up against practically every other country on earth (many of whom had probably never heard of football). And we were always top of both leagues. What's more, we won the English cup every spring regularly, competing in the final against whichever team actually won it in real life. It was as simple as that.

Only once did the Roman Rovers falter. That was when my Brother condescended to take part in a match one Sunday afternoon, saying, "If the Romans lost the cup final I bet you'd play the match again".

I was incensed. To think my integrity had been doubted. I hotly denied any such suggestion.

"The Romans are men of honour", I cried, "If they lose, they lose like gentlemen".

For gentlemen the Roman Rovers certainly were. At half time they used to do a quick change into evening dress and sit down to a banquet, a table groaning with the most scrumptious food ever devised. (In reality it was a home-made cooky I used to munch all by myself in the scullery).

"Righty-ho then", said my Brother, who was at a loose end and didn't know what else to do to pass the time. "I'll be the Roman's goalkeeper, and you can be the other lot".

And needless to say, the Roman's lost. My Brother let through a simple goal just to test my honesty.

I must admit I got a little excited, for as the Roman Rovers' representative he seemed to be making no effort to get on terms, and I could see the English cup, which we had never before lost, slipping from our grasp without a fair fight.

I no doubt bellowed a little louder than one should on a Sunday, and my Father suddenly appeared at the upstairs window.

It was Father's custom every Sunday afternoon to have a little nap in bed. He did the job properly, undressing and putting on his nightshirt which reached just below his knees. It was a luxury to which he looked forward the whole week, and woe betide anyone who disturbed him.

In consequence, he was not particularly complimentary, and my Brother, who persistently pandered to Father's wishes, was all for calling the match off. But I would have none of it. The whole future of the Roman Rovers was at stake. It was a matter of principle.

"Come on", I yelled to my Brother, when Father had disappeared and closed the window, "Play up. Don't take any notice of HIM".

It was a silly thing to say, for Father had incredibly sharp hearing. There was a minute's pause and then Father appeared again. This time at the scullery door, and he was inviting me inside.

"Just a minute Dad", said I, as though nothing untoward had happened. "With you in a jiffy".

"You will come *now!*", thundered Father encroaching into the garden sufficiently for his thin legs to be in evidence.

So, in actual fact, the game was never officially finished, owing to the Roman's brilliant young centre forward being on the injured list.

I can remember one other occasion only when a Roman Rovers' match was left unfinished, and that was brought about, in a sense, through an unfortunate chain of circumstances.

The lady who lived next door, a Mrs. Barber, had a bathroom installed in her house, and this caused much gossip and speculation. Bathrooms were only for the rich in those days, and Mother averred she was getting ideas above her station.

Her house was built on a different plan from our own. One side of it stretched side-on to our back garden. A nice big solid brick wall, a great temptation to a small boy with a ball in his hand. However, although I was allowed to throw my ball against our own brick wall (unless Father was having a nap), it was forbidden absolutely to fling the thing against Mrs. Barber's. This was quite understandable and I never on any occasion broke the rule.

The new bathroom was built on to this very wall. It jutted out facing us, with a large shimmering window made of a new-fangled type of frosted glass.

Mother didn't like it, not even when Mrs. Barber took her inside and showed her the workings of the hot water system and the snugness of the white porcelain bath.

We, ourselves, performed our ablutions in a tin bath which was hung up outside the house when not in use. The water was heated in the copper and transferred to the bath in buckets. On cold winter nights we took our baths in front of the fire, and very cosy it was too. My Brother would have his first and then I had mine (in the same water, of course). Mother and Father followed with the same ritual after we had gone to bed.

I don't remember what exactly the match was that caused my imagination to flare up into such a mighty turbulence. I do remember that for some reason it became essential for the ball to float in from my left, and I was highly excited at the prospect. Without realising what I was doing, I flung the ball with all my might at Mrs. Barber's wall, misjudged my direction, and it went slap-bang right through her new bathroom window.

The unbelievable part about it is, Mrs. Barber was at the time in the bathroom having a bath, and my ball hit her in a rude place.

Mrs. Barber was a kindly woman, and she liked little boys. She waylaid my Father on his return home from work that evening, told him all the details and begged him not to be too hard on me. So long as a new pane of frosted glass was paid for she would be quite satisfied, she said. "Please don't hit him."

So I escaped the thrashing, but my Money Lender's Purse took a terrible beating.

I nearly went out of business.

11

Boat Race Day

Boat Race day played a tremendously important part in our lives in those days, grown-ups as well as children being emotionally affected. For some long time before the actual event took place, the merits of the two crews were discussed at length, in the pubs, in the schools and upon the highways. Often fierce arguments arose and tempers were roused, much the same as happens nowadays at some of our soccer matches.

As the great day drew near, everyone, male and female, displayed their colours. It was quite rare to see a person without either a light or a dark blue rosette. I don't suppose many of them had any knowledge as to where the Universities were situated, but it mattered not. You made a choice very early in life as to which boat you were going to support and that was your lot for the rest of your life. It was not 'done' to be a turncoat. As soon as I was old enough to understand, I was to discover that my Father, my Mother and my older Brother were supporters of Cambridge. So I decided to support Oxford.

On the morning of the great event there was a kind of stillness in the air. Nobody spoke much. The errand boys stopped whistling. From breakfast time on, we boys would gather in little groups. Latest bits of gossip that had filtered through regarding the race would be discussed in distorted whispers.

"I've heard that number three is being changed in the Cambridge boat".

"What for?"

"Ill, or something".

"My Father heard a lady tell one of his customers last night that Oxford's Stroke had been took bad".

"Rubbish! You're only saying that".

"Bet yer!"

"Honour bright?"

"That's what the lady said".

"I don't believe it. It's all me eye and Betty Martin".

As the morning wore on the tension mounted. Small boys who sold newspapers in the street, and were usually looked down upon, became little tin gods overnight. They might be 'in the know'. Their friendship was craftily sought.

"Want a sucker?" someone would say as one of these V.I.P.'s passed by; and he would probably be offered a sweet via the hand (to offer the bag was unwise — he might take two).

"Heard anything?" he would be asked casually as he gobbled up the offering. Feeling his position acutely, he would do his best to justify it.

"Nothing official, but I did hear they made a false start and had to go back and start again". And off he would go to await the special edition that would give the result and perhaps a few preliminary details of the race.

The day my Father announced he was going to take us to Hammersmith to actually see the race rowed was a Red Letter Day indeed. It was seldom we had a day out together, when we did it was mostly on account of Father having had a turn-up (as he called it) with the gee-gees. Mother abhored gambling of any kind, almost as much as she abhored the suffragettes and their unladylike behaviour. She was strictly Victorian. She found it hard to keep abreast with the times, which were slowly (very slowly) changing. As, for instance her horror when she read of the Crippen case and his paramour Ethel le Neve cutting off her hair and wearing trousers.

"Fancy a woman going so far as to cut off her hair! A woman's crowning glory", she gasped, "and dressed up in a pair of men's trousers! They *must* be guilty of murder, both of them."

Women were still riding their horses "side-saddle", and even a female on a bicycle struck Mother as indecent.

In the same vein she condemned any form of gambling. So Father did it on the quiet. The awkward part came when his little flutter brought him in an unexpected windfall and his generous nature prompted him to share his joy with all of us. It invariably took the form of a fish supper in a restaurant. This was looked upon as a great treat and one of Mother's specials.

"But where did you get the money?" she would plague Father with, again and again.

"Eat your fish and don't ask questions", Father would tease her, winking boldly at my Brother and I. Eventually, of course, he would own up, but it always happened to be a special occasion. He found a shilling lying in the road and presumed his luck was in, so put it on a horse. He once went so far as to say he'd had a dream and saw a certain horse winning, so presumed it was a message from the Almighty. Mother fell for it, hook, line and sinker. But we boys didn't believe a word. There were dubious characters who stood about at street corners and who were, I believe, called "runners". They were each in touch with a bookmaker of some kind, and the usual method of backing a horse was to approach one of these men with a coin wrapped up in a bit of paper on which the name of the fancied horse was written. It was illegal to bet this way, but it went on quite openly and Father happened to be friendly with lots of these men, so we drew our own conclusions.

"He's such a lucky man", Mother would say, "He hardly ever backs a horse, but when he does, it always wins". And we wouldn't bat an eyelid.

The journey from Bromley to Hammersmith was tiring and hazardous. It involved about three train journeys and a long walk. But our spirits were such that we hardly noticed it. My eyes were red from want of sleep, for I had been too excited to drop off during the night. When we reached Hammersmith Bridge the size of the crowd frightened us. On crossing the road, Mother grabbed Brother Fred's hand and Father grabbed mine. Hurried arrangements were made as to where we would meet up should we get separated. Half-way across the road I spotted a pin, I made a dive to pick it up, and a great motor bus nearly ran me down. Father was furious. We had lost sight of Mother in the meantime and Father shook me roughly by the arm as I waited for the bus to pass so that I could have another go at rescuing the pin.

Everybody knew the adage, surely:—

See a pin and let it lay,
Be unlucky all the day.
See a pin and pick it up,
All the day you'll have good luck.

I believed the implication implicitly, even though I was never quite happy about the rhyme of the last line (after all, I was a song writer), and above the noise of the traffic I quoted it to Father in a loud voice. He was not interested, and said if I didn't move quick he'd give me a slap round the behind.

So the pin stayed where it was.

We found Mother after a while, and we made our way to the side of the river where we established a good vantage point. I think half the population of London visited the Thames to see the boat race in those days. We soon became tightly wedged, and then a huge boat pulled up right in front of us which blotted out a large part of our view. However, our excitement was not to be denied, and the longer we waited the more tense we got. After what seemed an age, we heard rousing cheers farther up the river.

"They're coming!", yelled the crowd about us.

"Who's winning?"

"Cambridge!"

"Well rowed Cambridge". The roar was enormous. Everyone around us seemed to favour the light blues. I was the only one with a long face. Father lifted me up on to his shoulder as the Cambridge crew slid past the small gap left by the huge boat directly in front of us. Father cheered, Mother cheered, everybody cheered. They rowed smoothly out of our sights, looking neat and smug. I could have thrown my boot at them.

There was a lengthy pause, and then Oxford hove into view. They seemed to be struggling. They were throwing up great sprays of water, and they looked worried.

"Come on Oxford", I yelled (solo).

My voice was drowned by the tremendous shouts of praise for Cambridge. Father removed me from his shoulder and we all sat down and waited. It was customary to hang about until the race was completed, and then a boat came back up-river hoisting a flag with the colours of the winner, and the man in it would hold up a number of fingers depicting the amount of lengths by which they had won. We heard the cheers long before we saw him. Cambridge, it seemed, had won by three lengths.

It was then it started to rain. We pushed through the crowds and made for home. By the time we got back to Bromley, we were all pretty wet and miserable. Even my Mother was tetchy, and I finished up with a good hiding and was sent to bed early.

"And all because of a little pin", I kept telling myself.

It was a long time before I forgave my Father.

12

Queer in the Choir

I began my life as a choir boy in St. Luke's Church at Bromley Common. A fine old church, known in devout circles as 'High Church'. The discipline as far as the choir was concerned was remarkably strict. I had just reached the age of seven and Mother, who had already got my elder brother accepted, took me along to see the choir master whose name was Mr. Wild (Wild by name and wild by nature some said). He was very young for such an important job and I realise in retrospect he must have been exceptionally clever, for St. Luke's had a large following of prominent local people. But he was an incredibly testy individual and not all that fond of small boys. He'd give us a clip round the ear as soon as look at us. I got through my initiation without any untoward enthusiasm on the part of Mr. Wild, and was taken on pro tem as a probationer. That meant I had to attend choir practice with the others thrice weekly and on Sundays I sat in the front pew facing the choir, much as a professional footballer sits on the side-line when he is a substitute, hoping for a drop out.

However, I had quite a decent singing voice, not perhaps all that sweet but intensely powerful, and it wasn't long before I was taken on as a full-timer. The fee suggested for my humble offering was two shillings and six pence per quarter. There were deductions for fines, and these I found were not hard to come by. Mother was delighted, and quickly got to work with a licked pencil as to how the cash should be spent, bearing in mind Brother's fee for the same period was four whole shillings. Further, Mr. Wild had pointed out to Mother that in due course, if we proved ourselves good enough, we could become soloists, in which case, the fee could rise to as much as seven shillings and six pence (minus fines of course, tho' he didn't say that).

Mother was ecstatic, and Brother Fred loved it all. I sang my heart out, but for some reason I invariably fell foul of Mr. Wild. Trouble was, nature had endowed me with an extraordinary desire to argue. My Father had noticed it, almost from the first. "His tongue will hang 'im!" my Father would reiterate when I'd beaten him to it with the last word. And Mr. Wild noticed it too. It wasn't so much that I wished to prove the other man wrong, but I think I must have had a querulous legal-type brain that needed to sort things out to the final detail. This, from a small boy, can, of course, be very tedious, and Mr. Wild found it so. Most of my fines were for arguing the point, but we could also be punished for a variety of reasons; turning up late for practice, chewing sweets in church, not singing loudly enough, sniggering, and so on. For all that, every quarter, the boys lined up expectantly and it was interesting to watch the faces fall as they held out their hand.

It always got up my nose on the first Sunday after to see Mr. Wild turn up in a brand new suit. I was convinced he had bought it on the proceeds of our fines. I used to glare at him and think, "You swine! But for me you would have only half a sleeve to that jacket".

All boys in those days were labelled with a nickname, and in many cases he was stuck with it for the rest of his life as far as his school chums were concerned, which was a pity really, because in most cases the name wasn't very flattering. There was Marrow Woodhams, Mousey Hewit, Jigger Reid, Punch Ludlow, Monkey Morrison, to give you an idea; and my Brother was called Molly — in connection with a popular song of the day, which went, "Molly O'Morgan with his little organ". I was let down rather lightly with Patsy, the name of a local policeman who died about the time we arrived in the Town. No connection between the two things as far as I knew.

One day an under-sized and very fragile little boy turned up for choir practice whose name, as far as we were concerned, was Jellyfish. There was every good reason for this, to be frank. His eyes, which were a kind of pale grey, blinked at you behind the most enormous spectacles and, to put it kindly, he was a little bit soft in the head. Weekdays he attended what was popularly called "The Silly School", and each morning he and a few others like him were picked up and taken to the school in what was termed "The Silly Bus". Boys, of course, are notoriously cruel one to the other. I don't think it ever dawned on any of us that this phraseology could be hurtful or harmful to anyone. One boy would address another with, "Here you, you go to the Silly School don't you?", and the other would probably reply with complete phlegm, "That's right, my sister goes there too".

So here was Jellyfish, ready and anxious for his first choir practice, having been accepted as a probationer.

At the conclusion of the practice, in which he had behaved impeccably, we got him to one side and we all went into a close huddle.

"Well done", we chorused with mock enthusiasm, "You got through with flying colours, but the Choir Master is very cross with you".

"What have I done wrong?" faltered Jellyfish nervously.

"You keep calling him Mister Wild", we said in a hushed whisper. "His right name is Mister Furious. We only call him Wild because he *gets* so wild. Best thing for you to do is go over to him right away and offer an apology".

Jellyfish blinked at us from behind his thick-rimmed

spectacles. He was not entirely convinced.

"We call him Mister Wild behind his back", we insisted sotto voiced, "But you've been calling him Mister Wild to his face. He's furious!".

"Is he?", queried Jellyfish. He turned and looked across to where Mr. Wild was irritably stowing bits of music in his case. He did a quick swallow, then minced over to him and said in his prim little way, "Excuse me, sir".

"Yes, what d'you want?" snapped Mr. Wild.

"I'm sorry if I called you Mister Wild just now, Mister Furious, and I hope I didn't make you wild doing it".

Mr. Wild looked up, paused for a second, then cuffed him soundly round the ear.

And that I'm afraid ended the career of Jellyfish as a choir boy.

In course of time, owing to a daily improving voice rather than to good behaviour, I acquired the honoured position of number one solo boy. I led the choir round the church at processionals, sat on a chair on my own at the end of the row facing the congregation, was given the choicest solo bits to execute, and in my prominent position was able to belt out the rest of it much louder and far more noticeably than the others. All this suited my ego to a "T". It is, therefore, quite extraordinary, when I look back, with all this success encompassing me like a halo, that what I am about to relate could very well have taken place.

I suppose, as usual, I had been cheeky and it was most likely a culmination of events that led to Mr. Wild suddenly coming to a decision that the choir might be better off without me for a couple of weeks. It was not unusual for boys to be suspended for an odd night or so, but it was almost unheard of for one to be laid off for two weeks, and more especially the head solo boy. But that's what happened to me. It was a dilemma of the first magnitude. But, as so often happens to naughty boys, God was on my side.

My Brother, a little to my surprise, didn't split on me at home, and each practice I toddled off with him and hung about outside the church hall until it was over, returning home with him as though nothing was up. Luck again prevailed when on the first Sunday of my suspension, my Mother was poorly with a cold and for once in her life missed the evening service. I was just congratulating myself on my good luck when fate, in the shape of my Father's Mother, did me a dirty trick.

My Father, to all who knew him, was looked upon as a brave man. The only time I ever saw him frightened was when someone mentioned his Mother. I, myself, had never met the old lady. She lived at Maidstone. She had given birth to fifteen children, thirteen of which still survived. My Father was the youngest but one. The youngest of all was my Aunt Minnie. She had never married because it had been borne in upon her at an early age that her lot in life was to stay home and look after her Mother, and not go careering off and getting married to some strange man.

So, when the postman, with a shart rat-tat at the door, brought a letter for Father saying his Mother would be calling for a cup of tea on the forthcoming Sunday, there was consternation extraordinary at our house. Father went sick in the stomach and turned exceeding pale.

"Cheer up, ducky", Mother kept saying, "We'll have a nice cup of tea and then take her a long country walk".

"I don't think she walks much now", Father said at last, "She's over eighty and very frail".

"That's all my eye and Betty Martin", Mother replied hotly, "Last time I saw her she was as strong as a horse".

"Minnie says", argued Father referring to the letter, "Don't bother to meet us at the station as Mother will be taking a cab". This bit of information caused quite a stir.

"It's over a mile", said Mother in a hushed whisper, "It'll cost her a shilling if not more".

"She's very old", Father kept saying; and I rather thought his voice had become weak and high pitched. Not his usual deep profundo, rather like a little boy's. And I do remember that very secretly, deep down and almost ashamedly, I was enjoying the situation, in a sort of sadistic way; little dreaming of what fate had in store for me.

We awaited the old girl's arrival on the Sunday with a mixture of feelings. Mother, in a sense, seemed to be rather looking forward to it. She adored company and no doubt was thinking of the nice chat, or it could have been that she, too, was just a little bit appreciative of seeing Father tamed in his own den as it were. Who knows?

I was fully instructed as to what part I would play in the proceedings. Call her Grandmother when spoken to, and when not spoken to, keep my big mouth tight shut. Rise when Grandma rose, not to collar the best chair, and wash behind my ears. Everything was all set and planned and Mother cheered Father up a bit with, "She won't stop long ducky, the last train to Maidstone is eight-something".

"That's true", agreed Father, brightening a little, "and she doesn't like the night air because of her rheumatism".

"Probably leave as soon as we've finished tea", Mother said, and then added, "I wonder what time they'll arrive".

We soon found out. Mother, in fact, was just washing up the mid-day dinner plates and we boys were leaving for Sunday School when we heard the wheels of a cab (known as a growler) draw up outside the house. Cabs were not often used as a means of transport in our road, and a small gaggle of children were gathering as I opened the front door in time to see my Grandmother give the cabby a penny tip.

Grandmother sailed in, and I was pushed unceremoniously to one side as Father gave his Mother a peck on the cheek and shook hands with Aunt Minnie. Mother then appeared up the hall, hastily wiping her hands, and joined in the happy reunion. Brother Fred was brought forward and kissed, with sundry remarks as to how much he had grown, and then I was introduced and we all made for the kitchen.

Grandmother had plainly modelled herself on the late Queen Victoria. Her hair, still ebony black despite her age, was parted severely in the middle and shone like a beacon. She wore a quaint little bonnet (called, I believe, a poke) and a black shawl. Her skirt was voluminous and obviously covered several petticoats, and she wore high-buttoned boots. When she spoke, which was pretty often, she delivered her opinions in a low-pitched rasping sort of voice, and somehow you just had to listen to her. In fact, she made quite sure that you did.

Father pottered about and got more clumsy every minute, and at a hint from him, which consisted of a sharp dig in the ribs with his thumb, we boys excused ourselves and made off for Sunday School.

By the time we returned things were more settled. The action had now moved to the sitting room, where, on the best table, the tea was laid out in grand style. Teatime in those days, and especially on Sunday, was a much bigger affair than it normally is to-day. Even the most humble homes indulged in a bit of a spread. There would probably be rabbit pie, apple tart, cakes, cheese straws — all newly made that morning, as well as a selection of jams and bloater paste, and quite likely some home-made bread. The silver teapot and the one good set of crockery would be on display as well as, in our case, the silver cutlery which was the last relic of Father's and Mother's wedding presents and only used on Sundays and Christmas Day.

We drew chairs up and got busy with the victuals and Grandmother had more time to inspect me. She was told that I was not very brainy but that I liked football. I had a nice singing voice they said and, on the whole, was a good boy but that I hated washing my neck. Brother Fred was, as with most of our relations, held in very high esteem. It was quite usual to put the first born on a pedestal, and my Brother could play the part to perfection with slight blushes and modest remarks, all beautifully timed at the right moment. He'd been at it all his life, and I envied him.

The tea-party went off much better, I think, than anyone had anticipated, the only tricky moment came when Grandmother slung back one of Mother's home-made buns saying she couldn't stand things with currants in. We all sat there expanding with good food and pleasant thoughts when quite suddenly, and without warning, Grandmother dropped a bombshell. She looked across at my Father with her penetrating dark brown eyes and said, "I suppose you still go to church, Rowley?".

"Oh yes, Mother", lied my Father, "Every Sunday, never miss".

"Good!" said the old lady, "Then we'll all go tonight. I'd love to hear the two boys singing in the choir."

My Father nearly fainted. He hadn't been inside a church since his wedding day, and hated it. But his dilemma was nothing as compared to the pickle I was in. The tense silence that followed her remark was frightening. My Father found his voice after a lot of throat clearing and said, "It's a lovely summer night for a walk. Pity to spoil it".

"Spoil it?" thundered Grandma, "Nothing could be more beneficial than an hour spent in the House of God. And I'm dying to hear the boys sing".

One of the boys was on the point of dying right there and then, but she didn't know it. I was conscious of a dull whining note going on in the back of my head. I have experienced it since during adult life when something really dreadful has befallen me. But at the time it was a new sensation, and in a mesmeric kind of way I was fascinated by it.

"Then we'll all go together", I heard my Grandmother say, in a voice far away. What to do? I knew not! We all got into our outdoor clothes and off we went. My brain refused to function, I couldn't think. Brother Fred and I lead the way, Mother and Aunt Minnie fell in behind, and Father and Grandmother, arm in arm, came up at the rear in stately fashion. The church hove in view and I had never known the walk to be so short. The grown-ups sidled off through the main entrance and I followed my Brother into the little ante-room which led to the vestry. My Brother gave me a pathetic look and disappeared through the vestry door. I was left to my thoughts, which, at the time, were not very clarified.

I hung about in the shadows, hoping no one would spot me. The thought did cross my mind once of going boldly into the vestry, seeking out Mr. Wild, explaining the whole fearful situation to him, and falling on my knees for humble forgiveness. But in my mind's eye I saw his thin little face crease up into one large satisfied smirk, and I knew instinctively I would be barking up the wrong tree. I was doomed, and the only hope was to play it by ear.

As mentioned before, St. Luke's was a 'high church' and liked to do things in a showy kind of way. The procedure at the commencement of the service was for the choir to enter via the vestry door, through the ante-room, parade along in front of the congregation, make a quick sweeping movement to the left up the aisle to some steps leading to the altar, and then fan out into their respective places either side.

The choir poured out through the vestry door and began to pass quickly by the dark recess where I was in hiding. It was now a case of quick thought and precipitous action. As the boys passed by, I nipped out from the gloom and tacked myself on to the procession. It must have looked odd, when I come to think of it, the choir personnel in their dark cassocks and lilly-white surplices, and me in the middle wearing my Norfolk suit and my washable celluloid collar, prancing along with them as though it were part of the production.

As we approached the aisle I was suddenly possessed with an insane idea of mounting the steps with the others and taking my seat in the usual way. Some cock-and-bull rubbish was racing through my brain about my choir gear having caught fire, and there wasn't another to fit me, so at the last moment . . . Then I caught sight of Mr. Wild, sitting high up playing his organ and glowering down at us behind his shimmering pince-nez! So, as the procession veered off to the left I did a solo turn to the right and wheeled round in the opposite direction finishing up without any conscious momentum on my part in the only vacant seat available — which happened to be right in front of my Father.

I could almost feel the staggered silence going on behind me as my Father leant forward to address me, but I was saved by the bell as the parson said, "Let us pray", and we all knelt down. Even then my Father tried to get at me, but his Mother shushed him. We rose at the end of the prayer and the organ played the introductory music for the first hymn.

"Why aren't you in the choir?" hissed my Father, and out of the corner of my mouth I hissed back, "Tell you later Dad", and then belted out at the top of my voice, "Oh, for the wings, for the wings of a dove". And never did any choir boy sing it with such verve or sincerity.

Strange to say, I never did have to tell him. It so happened that Grandmother missed her last train back to Maidstone, and we had to put her up for the night. What with the shemozzle created by Father and Mother turning out of their bed and sleeping in ours, and us having to have a temporary shake-down laid out on the floor in the kitchen, my little vagary was completely forgotten. I took good care to keep out of the way of Father for a couple of days, and the only one to really get the dirty end of the stick was my Brother.

Mother suddenly tackled him one day, without warning, and demanded to know the truth as to what had happened. Like the conscientious lad that he was he owned up, making a clean breast of the whole wretched business from start to finish. Mother was appalled! But she didn't seem to be so much upset about my part in the plot as the fact that Brother Fred had been deceitful by not telling her about it at the time.

"You of all people", she kept wailing, "I'll never trust you again, never".

Brother Fred stood there with tears trickling down his cheeks. And I got away with it Scot free.

13

Musical evenings

I was in my seventh year when I became obsessed with song writing. I had for some time been writing short stories, with the occasional full-length tale consisting of some five hundred words, and relations on both sides of the family were frequently presented with one of these epics as a birthday present, (whether they wanted it or not).

Music always fascinated me and the tonic sol fa which I learnt at school came easily. Further, my head was always filled with lovely tunes, and it wasn't long before I started jotting them down. I drew my own five-line staves on blank paper, and filled in the notes with pencil. The difficulty was, I had to work from my own middle C which existed in my head, and work out the positions of the other notes from there. Even after we had a piano I was not allowed to touch it, not so much because of the risk of damage but the expense of lighting had to be considered. So I had to work out my compositions in the kitchen, and it was an amazing coincidence that no sooner had I commenced composing than a member of the household would immediately start to hum something. This, of course, was most off-putting, and eventually I decided to use the outside lavatory as my music room. I would often spend the whole evening there writing music until the candle went out. I was fairly prodigious and turned out, on average, one a week.

It was the custom of my Uncle Fred and family to foregather at our house after tea each Saturday prior to weekend shopping in the Town, and it became a convention for me to get up and sing my latest creation. My Aunt Emily would begin her customary giggle even as I intoned the introductory bars, and as the song proceeded her laughter mounted until, having reached a stage of shrieking hysteria, she would be brought back to equilibrium with the aid of a dribble of brandy.

It always gave me a feeling of humiliation and hopelessness, but my Uncle Fred would goad me on with the promise of a whole penny to be given the moment the song was finished. So I would carry on, trying to make my voice rise above the increasing ridicule, my thrifty nature prompting me to accept the bait.

We were endowed with a large number of relations, and most of them had some kind of musical talent or were decidedly gifted in some other social sense. All were extremely good company for an evening out.

Musical Evenings, as they were called, were a frequent occurrence in our coterie. Any excuse was good enough, it might be a celebration or it might be just a case of a spontaneous desire for a get-together.

"What about us all meeting at my place next Sunday?" Father would say. "Bring your music Grace, and Frank will give us a turn on his flute, won't you Frank? And Alf, bring the old fiddle, boy. I'll get in some boose. Tell Eddy and the others".

And on Sunday some ten to twenty people would turn up all armed with their "pieces". Nearly all could do something, sing, recite, play an instrument or tell a good tale. We were never short of pianists either, indeed some of them could do a good "turn" at the piano as well as being an accomplished accompanist.

The majority of the older folk had a repertoire of just the one song. Seldom did they have music for this. The procedure was to wander over to the pianist, hum a few bars into his ear, and pronto, off we went. If he was a good pianist, not only would he vamp in perfect unison, he might even put in a few twiddley bits on his own account. But the evening was usually well advanced before the elders were sufficiently primed to get up and do their stuff. To put it their way, "they had to be in the mood". In other words, they needed a little alcoholic stimulant.

It is difficult to know, looking back, from whence came all their energy, for people worked long hours and our musical evenings went on invariable till the small hours. My Father, for instance, had to rise about 4.30 to be ready to commence his milk round at 5 a.m. It was nothing unusual for our parties to finish at about 3. Father would say, "Right, I'll have an hour's kip", and next day he would be as bright as a button. It also puzzles me where he got the money, for there was always plenty of beer and spirits, plus all kinds of "eats", and the customary lemonade-and-port for the youngsters. But then, so many things puzzle me about those times and the remarkable people who lived in them.

If it was winter time, and mostly it was, because long walks were the fashion during summer evenings, we would indulge in an enormous fire. Father looked upon it as his bounden duty to ensure nobody felt physically cold. He would potter in and out unobtrusively while someone was ripping off a song, and there would be, in addition to the pianist's accompaniment, the sound of much stoking and poking as an added bit of colourful background. The fire would crackle away brightly and Father would study it carefully; if it wasn't quite to his liking he would leave the room discreetly and reappear with an armful of logs. These he would pile on the flames until all present would be freely perspiring, and it would become necessary to open a window. The vocalist, whoever it was, would be imperturbed by these distractions and carry on regardless, even if (as on one such occasion) the carpet caught fire and the room filled with smoke.

My Aunt Grace from Maidstone used to impress me in particular at these musical functions. Completely self-taught, she was a brilliant pianist-accompanist, played the violin, the mandolin and the banjo, as well as having a delightfully tuneful singing voice. She also wrote music and had her own vocal choir in Maidstone which she conducted at all the festivals and eisteddfods all over the country, invariably pulling off the first prize. She made a good living teaching, using all her accomplishments for the purpose. She was my Father's eldest sister. She thought nothing of travelling up by train for these occasions, staying the night with us, and dashing back to Maidstone the next morning in time to get there for "her first lesson". She lived to be over ninety years of age, and only gave up her busy way of life shortly before her end.

There were some talented relations on my Mother's side too, by the name of Lightfoot. I'm not quite sure how they fitted in, second cousins or something. Five of them altogether, two played the piano, one played the flute and the other two were vocalists. And there was Aunt Polly who, in some way, was connected with them and whose age was in the high eighties. She wasn't particularly gifted but liked her drop of gin, and was wont to sing "Old Love Letters", in a sweet, but tremulous, voice, when she'd had some.

When Father got up to sing *his* number, we knew the party was truly under way. He would stand up, empty a glass, tap the pianist on the shoulder, and the next thing we knew he was singing his lively six-eight-tempo ditty which went like this:—

Wheel the perambulator John,
Be careful how you go,
Don't get wild, but mind the child,
And wheel it very slow.
When you turn the corner, going across the road,
Just lift the front wheels up a bit,
And don't upset the load.

He sang it with great gusto and we all joined in the chorus. He would then pour himself another glass with remarkable alacrity, and retire modestly to the background.

This would be the signal for my Uncle Fred to go lolling over to the piano and have a hurried consultation with the pianist, whichever one happened to be sitting there at the time, and next thing Uncle Fred would be singing and telling us about "The difference between East and West". It was a descriptive song, comparing the virtues of the East End Cockney with the depravity of the West End Toff. To say the lyric was a bit mawkish is to put it but mildly, but the melody was pretty and, taken at a steady tempo, was just right for community singing late at night. We all bawled it out in harmony, the obligato sometimes outdoing the melody, and my Uncle Fred waxed more sentimental as the song proceeded. Aunt Emily, who sat through the whole evening sewing garments and darning socks, would now shed a silent tear, her only contribution to the evening's entertainment.

There was one mysterious character who turned up without fail at all our Musical Evenings. His name was Mr. Bellows, and he was neither a relation nor even a close friend of any of us as far as I know. Yet, sure as eggs, as the evening got under way, there would be a ring at the front door bell and uninvited and unannounced, in would stagger Mr. Bellows; always merry, always polite, but never sober.

There would be cries of "Why, it's Mister Bellows", and the cosy armchair in the corner by the fireside would be vacated to accommodate him. He was given this particular seat with calculated prudence for, being nicely wedged in, he couldn't possible fall out. Nobody knew who he was or where he actually fitted in, but such was the social spirit of theday that he was shown (or helped) to his seat with the greatest cordiality and immediately asked "what he was going to have".

What amazed me at the time, and still does, is how he ever got to know when or where these affairs were scheduled to take place, for half the time we didn't know ourselves until the last minute. But he always turned up, an integral part of the ceremonies.

Round about midnight he would suddenly bestir himself, rise unsteadily to his feet, lurch over to the piano and supporting himself heavily on the pianist's shoulder would hum a few bars of music into his ear. The pianist, knowing his job, would rattle off a few arpeggios and Mr. Bellows would sing his number:-

A man is a man,
Says a very old saw,
And poverty is no disgrace,
For, a man is a man,
Whether wealthy or poor,
If his heart is but in the right place.

It had a sickly sentimental melody to go with the words, and, taken at a very slow pace, the chorus would be repeated many times for all present to join in.

It was also the signal for the refilling of glasses, including Mr. Bellows, who would somehow contrive to sing and sup up his drink simultaneously, whilst beating time with his half-emptied glass in between with such dexterity that he didn't spill a drop. Having finished the song he would drain his glass and submit to being half-helped and half-carried back to his armchair, where for the remainder of the evening he would settle down to the serious business of drinking whatever beverage was put in front of him.

The party would eventually break up and we would all gather on the doorstep for the final farewells. Then would come the hazardous problem of seeing Mr. Bellows safely home. Usually someone present knew where he lived and would volunteer.

"Leave it to me", a voice from the darkness would say, "I know where he lives, I'll look after him". As a general rule it was as simple as that.

But there came a time once at my Uncle Fred's house when as the evening, or perhaps I should say early morning, drew to a close there was no response to the puissant query "Who's going to see Mr. Bellows home?"

Nobody it seemed had an inkling where he lived, and it was a very dark night. So Uncle Fred felt it encumbent upon him, as it was his party, to become the gallant and see the indisposed gentleman safely to his front door. But finding his front door was not apparently quite as simple as all that. First of all, of course, it was necessary to find the right street.

My Uncle Fred had a whispered conversation with Mr. Bellows in the corner and withdrew to assure us that all was well.

"I know the place", he said with confidence, "I pass it on my way to work every morning. Give us a hand and we'll have him home in no time".

We saw them off and yelled goodnight to Mr. Bellows as he disappeared into the gloom firmly clasped round the waist by Uncle Fred. My Aunt Emily and her two girls prepared for bed as we all made off towards our respective homes.

Uncle Fred was not seen again until breakfast the next morning, when he turned up a little weary and still clutching the irrepressible Mr. Bellows round the waist. It appeared they had spent the night in and out of people's front gardens, my Uncle on his knees most of the time, striking matches in search of a small rosebush which Mr. Bellows insisted grew in his forecourt to the exclusion of every other house. Apart from running out of matches and being moved on by a policeman, nothing of any importance had taken place, and Mr. Bellows, after a hearty breakfast, settled down to a long sleep in the best chair, where he remained all day, waking up in time for another musical evening which was taking place in a house next door. The vital question of seeing him home then arose again. This time, however, we heard no more, so presume the garden with the rosebush was found.

Perhaps it had grown a bit in the meantime.

The Bromley Workhouse was situated three miles out from Bromley Common, at Farnborough to be precise. My Brother and I were members of the local boy scouts, and we had a musical section known as the Shortlands Glee Party. Every so often we would visit the workhouse for the purpose of entertaining the inmates.

There was no organised transport so we did it on foot, taking the stage properties on a thing called the trek cart. On one such occasion I had been a bit under the weather so it was decided to let me do the journey by motor bus. Because of this my Brother entrusted to me the care of his violin, impressing upon me the enormity of my responsibility.

I saw the others off, complete with trek cart, and then settled down outside Bromley South railway station to wait for a bus. The service was erratic and there was no guarantee that one would stop to pick up a passenger at any given point, especially if the passenger happened to be a small boy wearing a Badan Powell Scout hat and hugging a violin case under his arm.

Fate is often unkind to little boys, especially when they are on their best behaviour and trying to do good, and so it was not my fault when, as I boarded the bus, the violin flew out of its case and bounced several times in the gutter, making a few strange musical noises as it sent. I rescued it, and to my surprise (as extraordinary as it may seem) no damage appeared to have been done. So I stowed it back in its case and decided to say nothing about it.

Our pianist was named Miss Bottomly, she was an elder sister of our Scout master. She was a bit of a fumbler, and at these affairs she used to drape the crown of her hat with perky little Union Jack flag. I could never think why.

My Brother liked to make a grandiose entrance with the violin under his arm, and my job was to enter just ahead of him and deftly arrange his music copy on a wire stand which he had purchased from the Mart in Bromley High street for a shilling. It was a fragile and rickety contraption and on this occasion fell down no less than three times causing him to make a false entrance.

We were quite accustomed to my Brother making a few weird noises when he played the violin, so for a start we were not unduly concerned. But as he played on the noise got curiouser and curiouser, as though it were running out of steam. I suppose the accident had caused some kind of rupture to the bit that holds fast the pegs, causing a gradual slackening of the strings.

My Brother stuck it for a while then stopped playing and addressed his audience. He said he was afraid something had gone wrong with his violin (as if they hadn't noticed), and he much regretted he would be unable to continue with his piece. However, rather than disappoint them he would instead sing "Ora Pro Nobis" as a duet with his younger brother.

The younger brother, who was standing close by in the wings with one hell of a guilty conscience, then promptly stepped forward and bowed politely in response to the smattering of applause, which might have been meant for him and which on the other hand could of course have been because his Brother had stopped playing the violin.

We quickly cleared the stage while Miss Bottomly foraged through her pile of music, the Union Jack fluttering in the breeze caused by her exertions. We had not sung "Ora Pro Nobis" for a long while, and the reason was twofold. In the first place my Brother, who was approaching the age of fifteen, had been experiencing a few irregularities with his voice. One moment the cadence would be remarkably high the next time uncommonly low. Further, he had spotted me putting in a few over-dramatised actions in some of the emotional bits which he judged to be unnecessary and in bad taste in a purely vocal duet. So he had taken it out of our repertoire. My Brother had a small but sweet voice, so he always took the top line and I came in with the alto bits so as not to drown him completely.

All went well until the last verse, and then in an effort to reach an exceptionally high note my Brother's voice let off a great crack, not unlike that of a starter's pistol. It then plummeted down into the souls of his boots where it firmly remained for the rest of his life.

So, in a manner of speaking, he started the duet as a boy soprano and finished up as a basso profundo.

14

The Moving Pictures

The Moving Pictures, as we called them, first came to Bromley when I was about seven. They made their début at the Central Hall, and the performances took place on Friday nights. There were two houses, one at five o'clock for the children and one at seven for the grown-ups. The programmes lasted approximately one hour, and consisted of a succession of short films. Indeed some of them would last no longer than three or four minutes, and there would be an appreciable wait in between while the man in the box got busy threading the next reel.

The Central Hall was a vast place with a huge gallery encircling it. It was used mostly for political meetings and the like, and quite often a band concert would be held there too. But it also had a pronounced ecclesiastical leaning and the man who owned it belonged in some way to the church and was avidly religious. He was an elderly man and wore pince-nez spectacles to which was attached a long black cord. He was a man of extremely good intentions and loved to stand upon the platform making long speeches spouting about them. Unfortunately, he had the most dreadful impediment and it was quite impossible to understand a word he said. But I well remember the enthusiastic claps he got when he eventually sat down, not because we had appreciated what he said so much as the fact that he had at last finished. The film programme could then begin.

The operating box was a temporary affair, and was perched up at the rear of the gallery. I used to get a seat as close to it as possible so that I could see how it was all done. The lighting was effected by a stick of black carbon, about the size of a piece of chalk, which lit up the small box with a brilliant bluish-white light and had a blinding effect if you looked right at it. Occasionally it would burn low and the operator would push it up a bit; this would be reflected by the density of light on the screen. The screen itself was also of a temporary nature, it was in fact little more than a large white sheet weighted at the bottom to keep it taut. Any movement close to it would cause it to wobble, and the picture would go a little peculiar. We were not critical of such minor details. The very fact that the picture moved was enough to satisfy us.

As each small reel was finished the operator would place it outside for re-winding, his box being of limited dimensions. On account of this I was able to study the technique as to how the pictures appeared to move. It was so simple I could hardly believe it. I told my Brother about it; I told my Mother about it; I told lots of people about it. But no one believed me. So, to prove myself right, I set about editing a film on my own account. I drew a succession of pictures in pencil on the bottom of a hymn book in church. Each one was just that little bit different, so that when the pages were flicked over the overall picture appeared to move. This technique, in 'flicker' form, has, of course, been used in many ways since then, but at the time it was entirely my own idea, and I was middling proud of it. I can't say that anybody was particularly impressed, but at the time it thrilled me beyond description. In due course I pictorialised all the hymn books I could lay my hands on, during the sermon and other breaks in the church service. They consisted mostly of football matches with someone scoring a goal. Or it might be a boxing match with someone getting knocked out. Or an exciting race with a hectically close finish. Anything that inspired my sporting instincts was in course of time recorded in the hymn books of St. Luke's Church, Bromley. I have often wondered since what the effect must have been on the boy who eventually took my seat in the choir pew when he found what he had inherited. I can only hope that he had as much enjoyment out of watching the animated pictures as I got out of drawing them.

The Central Hall was situated close to the top of Bromley Hill, nearly three miles from where we lived. It was a long walk for small legs, and there was no public transport at that time. Yet, whatever the weather, we never missed. Every Friday, shortly after school hours, a swarm of happy-faced youngsters were to be seen all heading in the same direction. The Central Hall had become the centre of a new culture. But, as yet, only the school kids had caught on to it.

Then quite suddenly, the old Grand Theatre in Bromley High Street, which up till then had housed nothing more spectacular than stage dramas of the "Maria Martin" and "Sweeney Todd" kind, put up the shutters and announced that in future the Moving Pictures would take over. They would be put on once nightly with a full programme of films. A new firm moved in calling itself Jury's. The old Grand was given a face-lift and transformed into a picture house.

This was revolutionary indeed.

The grown-ups were sceptical. But the programmes were of a higher standard than those at the Central Hall, and would sometimes have a two-reeler as the star attraction. The films began to take on a more realistic angle, with interesting stories, love scenes, cowboys and Indians, exciting battles and lots of gooey pathos.

People began to go.

When they announced a showing of the famous story "Quo Vadis" in seven reels, all Bromley turned out to see it. Even my Father condescended, and grumbled volubly because he had to "line up" to get in (the word "queue" had not yet come into circulation).

124

THE MOVING PICTURES

It was the beginning of a new era. Very soon a place was built in the High Street, calling itself a cinema. Moving pictures were firmly on the map, and shortly to be called films. We watched with astonishment as the new building reached completion and gave itself the high-flown title of "The Palaise de luxe".

Most of us pronounced it as it was spelt, "The Palace de lux", but my cousin Daisy, who was seventeen and having French lessons twice a week, pronounced it the "Palyay dee Loo". And she twisted her mouth into all sorts of shapes when she said it.

That being as it may, the Palaise de Luxe put on programmes that pulled in the crowds from far and near, and it wasn't long before they engaged a pianist to play the piano while the films were in progress. I remember him well. A portly gentleman who hitherto had earned a precarious living playing in local pubs. He soon got into his stride and began to adapt his choice of music to the particular film that was being shown. If it was a comedy he would play something like "The Irish Washerwoman"; if it was something sad, he would rattle off a popular number of the day like, "If your heart should ache awhile never mind", and if it was a military scene, he would strike up a well-known march. The classic example came when a religious film was presented and we saw Christ walking on the water. He immediately struck up a few bars of "A life on the ocean wave".

Later on, all cinemas worthy of the name included a small orchestra to accompany the films, and in due course, a complete score of suitable music would be sent with the main feature film so as to give the right effect at the right moment.

The Palaise de Luxe was indeed a palace as far as we were concerned. We sat in plush tip-up seats and there were two programmes a night, Further, you could walk in any old time and leave when you felt like it. Which meant, of course, that you could, if you so desired, be in at the start and watch the programme twice through (which many of us did and suffered a tanning for getting home late). It was warm and cosy, and there was a small upper circle for those who didn't wish to mix!

The projector was discreetly hidden away behind the back wall up in the circle, and no longer could you see the man turning the handle. We became conscious for the first time of the strong beam of light that extended from the operating box to the screen. It was all so fascinating and mysterious. The screen, too, was no longer a piece of white material hanging from the ceiling, it was built into the wall, or so it appeared, and it was solid, so that no amount of movement could make it wobble.

It quickly became the custom to visit the cinema once a week. It was the "in" thing, or as we said in those days, it was "all the rage".

We learnt to discriminate. My Brother and I became infatuated with a funny little man who was just that bit different from the others. His tomfoolery had a "soul" we decided, and whereas we smiled and tittered at the other comics, we roared our heads off with laughter whenever this one came on the screen. We went to a great deal of trouble to find out who he was, for names were not very often given in the early days.

"He's called Charlie Chaplin", the manager at the cinema told us, a little surprised no doubt that one so young could be all that interested.

In due course we became confirmed addicts. We even visited a cinema when spending a day at the seaside. It was on the occasion of our annual choir treat. This was always a momentous event in our young lives. We looked forward to it, talked about it, and literally "lived it" for weeks ahead. A whole long day by the sea! I used to count the days.

The choice of venue used to be put to the vote, and we always, without exception, chose to go to Margate. It was traditional. We could not imagine ourselves spending the long-awaited choir treat anywhere other than Margate. Then, one year, for no reason other than someone suggesting a change, we decided by popular ballot to go to Ramsgate.

We assembled one bright summer morning, very early and very excited, and we boarded the train to take us to

Ramsgate. We arrived at Ramsgate Station, had a quick look at the seafront, then the whole lot of us boarded a tram and took ourselves off to Margate, here to spend the rest of the day in the familiar surroundings we knew and loved so well.

The tram dropped us off at Margate right outside a nice new cinema that had but recently been built. My Brother and I paid our money and walked straight in, like a couple of mesmerised rabbits. The programme was almost ended when my Brother leaned over to me and whispered, "Don't tell Mother we spent half the day in the picture house, she'd think us a couple of darn fools". Reluctantly we came out, about two minutes before the finish.

There were many traditions wound up with a day's outing at the seaside, such as taking home a present for your parents, playing pranks all the way there and singing songs all the way back, but the most important of all was to select a large hunk of seaweed from the seashore and take it home as a souvenir. It was hung up in a prominent place and used quite seriously as a weather prophet. The wireless had not yet been invented, and official weather forecasts hadn't even been thought of. So each morning the seaweed would be inspected; if it felt crisp and dry we considered we were in for a fine day; if inclined to be damp and clammy, rain was prophesied. A popular song of the day went: "As soon as I touched my seaweed, I knew it was going to be fine".

But, to revert to the cinema, a big boon was created when the motor omnibuses began to run regular services. People who lived in outlying districts were now able to go. Not that the buses in the early days were all that reliable. There were no timetables and no specific halts. You stood about on the kerbside till one hove in view and then wave your arms about and shouted. If the bus driver was a decent fellow, he would pull up and if he didn't like the look of you, he wouldn't. It was as simple as that. What's more, there was no guarantee you would reach your destination even when you got on a bus. They had a nasty habit of "breaking down". They were also reluctant to climb hills. It was nothing unusual, when half way up a steep hill, for the engine to give a languid splutter and stop dead.

"All out!" the conductor would shout, "Wait for us at the top of the hill".

So while you struggled up the hill, the bus, now bereft of passengers, would get going again and slowly snake its way up to the top.

It was not entirely unknown for a bus, having once got itself going, to continue on its way and not stop at the brow of the hill for fear it wouldn't start again. In that case you arrived there yourself, breathless and busless.

It was all part of the gamble.

Inside the bus you sat sideways, facing each other, with your feet in a very vulnerable position when the conductor came along to collect the fares. The top of the bus had no covering, which was a delightful prospect on a fine day. Later on, a small mackintosh sheet was attached to each seat, and this you could pull across your middle when it rained. Your head and shoulders, however, were still exposed. So, too, was the driver of the bus, for built-in cabins had yet to come.

For a long time a bus ride was looked upon as a novelty, and regarded as a luxury. It was a popular custom to spend a free day riding about on the top of a bus. Our turn came when Father one day announced that he had been given a holiday and intended taking us out for a day in the country.

"I thought we'd take a bus to Blackheath common", he said, trying to keep the excitement out of his voice. "Pop into Lewisham Hippodrome on the way back. Marie Lloyd's doing a turn there. How about it?"

Mother got busy making sandwiches and, after a reasonable wait, we boarded a bus. It was a glorious day and we settled down comfortably on the top deck; but Mother said she felt frightened every time the bus lurched over; she felt sure it was going to topple us all into the road. So she clambered down the stairs and went inside; and I went with her to keep her company. Actually, I was as scared as she was, but I wouldn't admit it, even to myself.

Then it began to rain, and Father, plus a lot more passengers on the upper deck, decided it would be more cosy inside the bus.

"Bloody people", grumbled the conductor, "When it's fine weather they all wants to go on top. When it's wet the silly sods all wants to go inside". Which, even at this distance of time, strikes me as being reasonable and realistic.

Father at the time happened to be smoking his large calabash pipe, and when he sat down inside the bus he was still smoking it.

"No smoking inside the bus", yelled the conductor.

Father pretended not to hear, so the conductor advanced into the middle of the bus and stood there regarding him.

"Didn't you 'ere wot I said?" enquired the conductor.

"Yes, I heard you", said Father politely, blowing a great cloud of smoke into the air.

"You can't smoke inside the bus", said the conductor loudly.

"Who says I can't?" countered Father.

"The law says you can't", emphasised the conductor.

"I think you are mistaken", Father replied, "the law says nothing of the sort".

So, at the first opportunity the conductor stopped the bus and hailed a policeman. There ensued a short confab between the two of them, and then the policeman clumped into the bus and stood there facing Father in a legal manner.

"What's all this about you smoking inside the bus?" asked the policeman.

"What's to stop me?" enquired Father, puffing away.

"It's the law, that's what stops you", said the policeman, raising his voice a little.

"I think you'd better look up your law book; page so-and-so. You'll find it under the Common Carriers Act 1830", said Father, and then went into a flurry of legal jargon, citing section this, and sub-section that. He held his bus ticket up and waved it about.

"This ticket is a contract", he said, "a contract between myself and Tilling's Bus Company, it is subject to current regulations and bye-laws, and no other terms may be imported into it. Right? This bus is a public vehicle travelling under the jurisdiction of the original Highway Code, as laid down for stage coaches, cabs, waggons, omnibuses, steamboats, lightermen, hoymen, barges, ferry boats, canals and river craft".

He went on and on, quoting legal technicalities, whether on rails, off rails, on wheel, without wheels, horse driven, steam driven, or mechanically propelled.

Which, when it was all boiled down, meant he could smoke inside the bus if he wanted.

The policeman reeled under the impact.

"I'll have to take down your particulars", he said at length. "Your name and address please?"

Father supplied the information and the driver of the bus re-started the engine.

"You'll hear more about this", was the policeman's parting shot as he jumped off the bus.

"I don't think so", said Father placidly.

And, sure enough, he never did.

Just how much he was within his rights I am not qualified to say. But I have been told that, at the time, the law on this matter was a little hazy. It was amended (so my informer says) in such a way that a person breaking the Company's rule of non-smoking, could be prosecuted for a "breach of the peace". In other words, a passenger could be *requested* not to smoke, but there was no law to enforce it.

Father smoked all the way to Blackheath.

Every now and then he would emit a little chuckle. As far as he was concerned the incident had made his day.

We hadn't the heart to tell him it had completely spoilt ours.

15

Epilogue

People sometimes ask me how different do I feel now that I am old; how differently do I "think"; what are the fundamental differences in life to-day, and in particular, how different are the children?

And the answer is, in each case, "There ain't none."

I still feel and "think" in exactly the same way that I did in my youngest childhood days. There just isn't any difference at all. I still sit and muse over things as I did when I was two, I still wax sentimental at the sight of a pretty little girl as I did when I fell in love with Red Riding Hood at the age of four, and when I am writing I still get into tempers with myself when I can't think of the right word, just like I did when I used to lock myself in the toilet to write my books and compose my music at the age of seven. No difference at all. The same old brain, same old "feel".

Fundamentally life has changed very little. People, I think, are very much the same deep down. They are more travelled, more worldly, and more tense. I think people in my childhood days were much more easily pleased. They were a happy breed. They had bags of time on their hands, and to be happy you must have plenty of time. On the other hand, people had very few possessions and very little money. Yet they seemed to do a lot with it. Contrary to what some politicians would have us believe, working class people ate much better than they do to-day, all excepting the *very* poor. Everyone polished off a good hot breakfast, a good midday meal, a good tea at about five o'clock and, almost always, a good hot supper. The food was plain but nourishing; adulterated food had not yet arrived and I doubt if anyone would have eaten it if it had. The midday meal was always called "dinner". Only the rich had "dinner in the evening". There were no cereals, and children ate very few sweets. Apart from the fact that parents couldn't afford them, it was considered bad for children's health. We did, however, always have "sweets" after midday dinner, it was considered an integral part of the meal, but it was not called a sweet, it was universally dubbed "the pudding". From a child's point of view it was the best part of the meal. Many a child would be threatened, "If you don't eat your meat you shan't have any pudding".

Any other changes? Let me think!

Yes, the air in those days smelt much sweeter. It could, of course, be the deficiency in an old man's odoriferous faculties, but I'm more inclined to think it has something to do with petrol fumes. Flowers seemed to have a much more penetrating smell, and there were hundreds of them growing wild all over the place. I miss the butterflies too. In the summer the air was teeming with them. We cruel little so-and-so's used to catch them in nets and when dead, pin them on to pieces of cardboard. The idea was to get a bigger collection than the chap next door, rather like collecting fag cards. There were dozens of difference species of butterflies, all very colourful and beautiful; as well as dragonflies, bloodsuckers, and daddy-longlegs.

"What do you miss most?" young people are apt to ask.

Well, one thing I miss in particular is the clanging of the school bell. It had a cosy, reassuring effect. Twice a day it rang out, and it went two times on each occasion. The first about five minutes before school time, and then "second bell" as it was called, on the hour; after which the doors were closed. If you were late you had to wait in the cloakroom, and after prayers you were given the cane (one stroke on the right hand). That's if you were a boy. Girls were given lines to write out after school hours, and they didn't go home till they had finished them. The original reason for the school bell was because many homes possessed neither a clock nor a watch, and the wireless had not, as yet, been invented. People judged the time of day by various noises, and the school bell was one of them. There were no school meals, although some pupils who lived a long way off would bring sandwiches to school and eat them in the playground. The hours were from nine till twelve, and then from two till half-past-four.

I miss the exhilarating whistle of the errand boys. Every one of them whistled. In fact, everybody either whistled or hummed a tune as they went about their daily work. The popular songs of the day were tuneful and simple, easy to commit to memory. I think the melodies had a relaxing effect. People were hardly ever tense, and they seemed to get a lot of fun out of their job however irksome or boring it might be.

I miss the sight of a drunken man, reeling about from side to side on his way home. This is a good miss of course, but it was a very familiar sight when I was a kid, especially at weekends. Nobody thought much about it, a bit of a giggle really, unless the drunk fell down and couldn't get up again. Then the police moved in, albeit reluctantly. If the policeman couldn't yank him off to the station by brute force, the ambulance was sent for, and he was pushed there in the little two-wheeler-with-the-hood-on-top. This kind of behaviour was very much looked down upon, it was comparable to washing your dirty linen in public. Decent people would pull themselves together, after a few drinks, and make for home quick.

I so well remember one Christmas morning when I was just eight. Several relations and friends had gathered at our house where the midday feast was being held. While the women were preparing the meal the men took themselves off for a drink at the local.

"Get them out of the way", said the women jovially.

It was the custom, in fact it was essential, for every man to "Stand his whack". As there were about a dozen of them this meant by the time the last half-pint was downed, they were getting more than a little tipsy. Father then said, "What about a Gin and It? Give us an appetite for our Christmas dinner". They all agreed, seeing that it was Christmas and the time to be merry. So they had about twelve Gin and It's, and by the time they reached home, none of them had any appetite for Christmas dinner or anything else. They were laid out in various parts of the house in a variety of postures, each with a bucket close at hand so that he could be sick in comfort.

Another good miss is the enormous hats that the ladies used to wear, perched up high on their heads and worn very, very, straight, which would obscure your view completely at any form of entertainment. At most concerts a gentleman would appear in front of the curtain just before the show began and say, "Would ladies kindly remove their hats!" And when silent films got going the same request would be shone up on the sheet. Some ladies would conform to the request and some wouldn't.

"Upset my hair, my dear!"

So if you sat behind one of those, you spent the evening dodging this way and that in the hopes of getting an occasional glimpse of what was going on.

I think people were better conversationalists than they are to-day, even the less literate ones. They could all illuminate their remarks with catchy phrases and idioms, and on the whole people seemed to have a better command of words. Further, people liked talking. They hadn't yet become conditioned to sitting mute while watching television and films.

Children have altered little, as far as my memory goes. The main change in the average child is, I think, that we were perhaps a bit more self-reliant. We were also more imaginative in our games. The reason is, of course, that nowadays so much of a child's leisure is "organised". Whether that's a good thing or not I am not qualified to say.

One thing I will say, at the risk of being hounded out of the country by admiring mums, I do believe that little girls on the whole were "prettier" than they are to-day. In an essentially feminine way, more delicate-looking and winsome. Their style of clothes was feminine too, with lots of petticoats and thick woollen combinations which were covered by long drawers with lace round the edges. They always wore hats in the street, and some of them gave the girl an added attraction. They all had long hair, and as a general rule, wore plenty of hair-ribbon to go with it. No little girl ever wore trousers. Unisex had not, as yet, raised it's hoary head. Girls were girls and boys were boys.

Boys wore short trousers and short hair. No boy at that time would have been found dead with long hair. Short back-and-sides was the fashion for both boys and men. It was "all the go", and considered very smart. I think perhaps boys were a little tougher than they are to-day, or at least we tried to be. We were weened on the stiff upper lip principle. Boys didn't cry. If they did they got precious little sympathy. As, for instance, when my Aunt informed me my Mother was not after all going to visit us at Leigh-on-Sea. I burst into a torrent of broken-hearted tears, whereupon my Aunt and the others made a circle round me and, wagging their forefingers under my nose, sang "Wee, wee, baby".

I soon stopped.

We were anything but angels however. I remember once leaving a note for my Mother saying in effect that I had left home. It was washing day, and we had had our usual little fracas; Mother was always tetchy under the strain. So, having failed to get my own way over whatever it was, I stalked out of the house, having first written a short note which said, "Goodbye, have gone for ever".

On my return from school, Mother opened the front door about two inches. I could just see her nose and one eye.

"Yes", she said, "What do you want?"

"It's me," I said, taken aback a little, "I live here".

She opened the door another inch, so that I could see the other eye. "You don't live here", she corrected.

"Yes I do. It's me!" I shouted, as she was about to close the door.

"I understood you had gone for ever," she said. For a moment I couldn't think what on earth she was talking about. "Oh that!" I replied casually, trying hard to think. "Yes, well, as a matter of fact . . . I've decided to give you another chance."

And having been thus forgiven she opened up for me to enter. A large fire was warming the room and there was a delightful smell of toasted bread. A plate of shrimps was gracing the lily-white tablecloth, a new pot of my favourite strawberry jam, a jar of dripping and, yes you've guessed it, a great hunk of Madeira cake!

I sat down, and I don't think I could remember ever having enjoyed a meal so much. My Mother sat in a dark recess and watched me gobble it up. I think she realised she had got a problem on her hands.

Sex was a subject that was absolutely taboo where children were concerned. I can hear the "moderns" clicking their tongues. But I'm not so sure. I don't think it did any harm. The overall effect was that boys respected girls with an almost saint-like attitude. Girls were a mystery. Sex was a mystery. Life was a mystery. I sometimes think (in my harrowing old age, of course) that once you've lost the mystery of life you've lost all.

For myself, I didn't know the facts of life until I was close approaching school-leaving age. Even then I didn't believe what I was told, and I got the whole thing out of perspective anyhow. Yet I was an incredibly sentimental little boy. I used to fall in and out of love every other day of the week. But, of course, the girls in question never knew it. I worshipped from afar off. I remember once buying an old cast-off ring from my Mother, I gave her a penny for it. She was curious to know for what purpose I required it. But I was very cagey.

The girl in question was in my class at school. At the time I was the class monitor, and on my way round the desks, handing out pens and other utensils, I would hang about when I got to her desk, and drop things, just to be near her. I didn't ever speak to her, I didn't even look at her. But I was emotionally aware of her. Her name was Vera Brooke, and one day in the school playground, in the middle of having a tustle with another boy, Vera passed by. I disentangled myself from my opponent and thrust the ring into her hand.

"Here you are", I said, "Want it? You can have it".

And then went on with the scuffle. That was my way of proposing.

My Mother was a very sentimental woman. I vividly recall the morning after Bleriot had flown the channel. For some time there had been great rivalry between he and Hubert Latham. It was a toss-up as to who would do it first. Amidst all the excitement of the great achievement the Daily Mirror showed a picture of Latham, with his head in his hands, shedding a tear in his anguish of disappointment.

"Oh dear", said Mother, "Fancy a man crying. He *must* have been upset", and then promptly burst into a flood of tears herself.

She loved the works of Marie Corelli and Ethel M. Dell. She would read bits out to us, absolutely living the romances, especially the pathetic bits.

Father was a different cup of tea. Completely unemotional. The only thing he read, apart from his daily paper, was John Bull. This was edited by a man called Horatio Bottomly, and to my Father he was a god. The paper was very political and full of legal intrigue. It was a weekly publication, and my Father read it from cover to cover at the weekends. Bottomly was notorious for showing up people in high places and getting the law to catch up with them. Unfortunately for him, the law, in later days, also caught up on Horatio Bottomly, and exposed him for the old humbug he was. He finished up with a seven years' stretch. But there's no doubt my Father gleaned a lot of his legal perception from his paper. For a self-educated man, Father's knowledge about most things was quite extraordinary. But he was very sensitive about his lack of education, and especially the deficiency in his manner of speech. We had to be very careful not to let him see us laughing when he made a slight faux pas of any kind. The four of us were once walking along Bromley Broadway, it was a lovely summer evening, and suddenly overhead flew an enormous bird. Quite low, it languidly flapped its way across the sky and disappeared. There was much speculation as to what it was. The general concensus of opinion alleged the bird to be an eagle. But Father would have none of it.

"If you ask me", he said, "in my considered opinion, I, personally, speaking myself, would say it was a n'awk".

We walked on in silence. We didn't laugh, we didn't even breath. We just walked, arm-in-arm, all four of us. In silence.

Quite suddenly my Father stopped. With the unexpectedness of the move my Brother and I, who were on the outsides, careered into each other almost bumping heads. My Father unlinked his arms and struck a theatrical posture. Then in a voice which he normally used for addressing public meetings he said,

"All right! Since you are so bloody particular ... *AY 'AWK!"*

To see a motor car was a novelty, and to be taken for a ride in one was an unforgettable experience. I had just joined the Badan Powell Boy Scouts when my chance came. A gentleman of high degree who was interested in the Scout movement and was the owner of a "motor", offered to take my Brother and I for a "little spin" round the country lanes, just to see what it was like. His wife said, as we clambered into the car, "Don't be nervous, now! My husband is a very good driver". Riding in a motor car was looked upon as an experience fraught with danger.

But if cars were a novelty, aeroplanes were a rarity. On the very few occasions one flew overhead, it was a sensation, and everyone stopped work to look at it. There was always the risk that it might fall down. Sometimes the engine conked out and it did. Yet the aeroplane must have made fantastically quick strides for it was only two years after Bleriot flew the channel that an "Aerial Derby" was widely publicised by one of the daily papers. The newspaper in question was arranging the whole thing and giving what was then an enormous prize to the winner.

I rely entirely on my memory, for I can find no record of this event in the reference books, but I believe I am right in saying the race was to take place from Hendon to Biggin Hill. Anyhow, Bromley Common was one of the places sighted as being a good vantage point to see the race, and as it was held on a Saturday afternoon, hundreds of people turned up from all over London. The Common at Bromley in those days really was a Common. Miles and miles of open meadow land. We, of course, were there, elbow to elbow with the madding crowd. To see one plane in the sky was a thrill, but over twenty had entered for this competition, and we had visions of them belting along, wing-tip to wing-tip, all straining at the leash like the competitors at a horse race. We were breathless with excitement.

We waited an age, and nothing happened. Then, all at once, we heard people in the distance shouting, "Here they come".

We craned our necks and screwed up our eyes. In the distance we espied what looked like a small boy's box kite. It hovered towards us and disappeared. After about ten minutes another one, which looked for all the world like a fragile little bird, hove into view and we waved to the pilot as he whizzed by overhead. Shortly after that another one appeared. And that was our lot.

The rest of them couldn't get off the ground.

The big thrill of the day came later. A poor old cart horse got himself stuck in a small pond and was slowly sinking in the thick mud. We watched in horror as the filthy water reached his head. Several men, fully clothed, waded in with a long piece of rope which they eventually tied round the horse's middle, and then the great feat of strength began. It took the best part of an hour, but when the rescue was complete, the crowds cheered and cheered. Father, for once in his life, showed some emotion. He adored horses. He stood there with tears in his eyes.

"Isn't it rum", he said, "they invent motor cars and machines that fly in the air, but it's a horse that steals the thunder every time."

One bright July morning in 1910, my Brother and I were awakened very early by our Mother. She stood at our bedroom door with the sun streaming in behind her, furnishing her with a kind of halo.

"Get up you boys, at once", she whispered, "The King's dead".

Even at the time I wondered what we could do about it, and personally I felt in no way responsible. But we stumbled out of bed and followed her downstairs. It was about five o'clock, and Father had just left for work. Mother generally got up and waved him goodbye from the upstairs window. It was then, on this occasion, she had spotted the placard outside the newspaper shop opposite: KING EDWARD DIES.

She was still in her long flannelette nightgown, and we were both in ours. Mother made a pot of tea, and we sat about trying not to yawn.

We talked in low whispers, and after a bit Mother got up and made another pot of tea.

One by one we drifted back to bed, there to finish our broken night's sleep. But Mother could think and talk of nothing else for a long time to come.

"The loss of the old Queen was bad enough", she said, again and again, "but this is terrible! I don't feel the old country will ever be the same again".

And to a certain extent, I think she was right.